T0001486

POCKET **ROUGH GUIDE**
LIVERPOOL

Written and researched by
DANIEL STABLES

CONTENTS

LIVERPOOL

From The Beatles to Bill Shankly, Liverpool has been the cradle of some of the United Kingdom's most iconic musical, sporting and artistic powerhouses. Enduring a bruising postwar period of economic hardship and urban deprivation, Liverpool turned a page with the coming of the new millenium. Today it is a thriving city, with sleek high-rise apartment buildings and fancy restaurants, great museums and galleries and a trove of listed buildings. But the old pillars – football, culture, and a gritty, can-do attitude, forged on the docks and in the warehouses – remain at its beating heart.

A sparkling view of Liverpool's waterfront

Liverpool, like its neighbour and great rival Manchester to the east, grew both rich and poor on the spoils of the Industrial Revolution. While working people toiled in the warehouses and factories, vast wealth flowed through the city's Custom House and into the pockets of the elite; for a time in the 19th century, Liverpool was fêted as the 'Second City of the British Empire' and the 'New York of Europe'. After the World War II, however, Liverpool saw a downturn in its fortunes which even the cultural vibrancy of the Merseybeat scene – best encapsulated by the worldwide phenomenon that was The Beatles – could not arrest. Manufacturing slumped, and by the 1980s Liverpool was among the most deprived areas in the United Kingdom. By the turn of the 21st century, however, things had begun to look up. Tourism has flourished in recent years, fuelled by a passion for football and the city's rich musical heritage, and striking works of modern architecture continue to spring up on Liverpool's iconic waterfront skyline, a foil for the stately Three Graces.

Nowhere better encapsulates the grit and grandeur of 19th-century Liverpool, and its modern regeneration, than its waterfront. Here you'll find the Albert Dock, Britain's biggest collection of Grade I-listed buildings; once

The Central Library

home to valuable stores of tobacco, silk and sugar, it now houses the contemporary art of Tate Liverpool, the exhibits of the Merseyside Maritime Museum, and a museum dedicated to the city's favourite sons: The Beatles. The legacy of the Fab Four looms large here, and the superb Beatles Story and Magical Mystery Tour are unmissable for fans – in fact, a Beatles pilgrimage is the main draw for many visitors.

Liverpool's rebirth continues apace just inland, in the Ropewalks district. Once, the warehouses and factories here made ropes for the

What's New

Nowhere better encapsulates Liverpool's 21st-century regeneration than the Baltic Triangle, an exceedingly trendy district of industrial warehouses and factories transformed into the modern creative and digital hub of the city. Touring bands and DJs grace the stage of *Hangar34*, while the achingly cool *Camp & Furnace* – part restaurant, part bar and part music venue – has to be the best spot in town for a Sunday roast. The Ropewalks area is another symbol of Liverpool's post-industrial rebirth. Once a rope-making district, today it's home to some of Liverpool's finest cultural institutions, including FACT, where you can catch indie films and rotating art exhibitions, and the Bluecoat, which hosts art workshops, poetry evenings, dance performances and more.

When to Go

Though it has seen some extreme storms, flooding and snowfall in recent years, Liverpool has a generally temperate, maritime climate, which means largely moderate temperatures and a decent chance of at least some rain whenever you visit. If you're attempting to balance the clemency of the weather against the density of the crowds, even given regional variations and microclimates the best months to come to England are April, May, September and October.

city's sailing ships; today, these historic streets house trendy food markets, the cutting-edge FACT cultural complex, and some of the city's best beer gardens and live music venues. Catching a band or artist, whether established stars or open-mic up-and-comers, is a must in Liverpool. Most famous of the city's venues is the *Cavern Club*, where John, Paul, George and Ringo cut their teeth in the early Sixties; you'll still find live music here most nights of the week. Rock and folk artists grace the stage of the *Arts Club*, while jazz echoes down the street from *Fredriks* and *The Grapes* – the latter another former haunt of the Fab Four. The Philharmonic

Hall, meanwhile, welcomes the classical world to its stage.

Multiculturalism runs deep in Liverpool; both the oldest black community in the United Kingdom and the oldest Chinese community in Europe have their home here, and the city's reputation for tolerance and inclusivity abides. North of Chinatown, Liverpool's wartime hardships are laid bare at the husk of St Luke's Church, its roof and interior lost to the bombs of the Blitz. To the east, elegant Hope Street represents the zenith of the stately 18th-century architecture of the Georgian Quarter; its mansions now house fine restaurants, great bars, and the Liverpool Cathedral.

Port of Liverpool Building

Where to...

Shop

Whether you're looking to splurge on designer clothes and jewellery, browse the best of the high street, or seek out one-of-a-kind antiques in quirky vintage stores, Liverpool can deliver your kind of retail therapy – there's a reason this is one of the most popular shopping destinations in the UK. The opening of the behemoth Liverpool ONE shopping centre in 2008 changed the face of the city centre, bringing every department store and designer fashion outlet you could think of to within a short walk of Liverpool's central train stations. Bold Street in Ropewalks has some less mainstream offerings, and is a great place to browse for one-off finds in independent vintage stores and dig for rare second-hand vinyl records. Bohemian Lark Lane, meanwhile, has its own share of vintage and bric-a-brac shops alongside witchy emporiums and independent art galleries.

OUR FAVOURITES: The Amorous Cat Gallery, see page 91. Dig Vinyl, see page 65. Gasp, see page 91.

Eat

Liverpool's burgeoning food scene makes it one of the most exciting places to eat in the country right now. This is another area in which Bold Street scores highly; in between the vintage boutiques and record shops are some of the city's very best restaurants, making a cosmopolitan scene with Indian, Middle Eastern and Italian cuisines all well represented. Liverpool also excels in high-end modern British cuisine, a concept which some foreigners may scoff at, but is establishing itself a position on the international scene which is too strong be ignored. Mention must also go to Liverpool's Chinatown, which as the oldest in Europe also has one of the best-established food scenes, whether you're after Cantonese or Szechuan.

OUR FAVOURITES: Maray, see page 66. Mowgli, see page 55. Mr Chilli, see page 66.

Drink

Even by the lofty standards of Britain's big cities, Liverpool does drinking and nightlife well. There are cosy pubs where you can curl up on a winter's evening with a local craft beer, elegant wine and cocktail joints perfect for kicking off a classy night on the town, and rooftop champagne bars affording unrivalled views over Liverpool's ever-evolving skyline. If you're after an unashamedly cheesy club night, all gummy carpets and chart tunes, there are plenty of them to choose from too. Increasingly, though, Liverpool is coming into its own at the opposite end of the spectrum, with an expanding array of arty, if self-consciously cool, venues which play the joint role of bar, music venue, and events space – the best of these can be found in the converted warehouses of the Baltic Triangle.

OUR FAVOURITES: Alma de Cuba, see page 67. Camp & Furnace, see page 67. Polidor 68, see page 94.

Liverpool at a glance

Cavern Quarter and around p.50.
The Beatles' famous former haunt is the centrepiece of this buzzing district of bars, restaurants and nightclubs – an absolute must for music fans or anyone interested in pop culture.

EVERTON

VAUXHALL

ISLINGTON

KNOWLEDGE QUARTER

ROPEWALKS

CHINATOWN

GEORGIAN QUARTER

BALTIC TRIANGLE

TOXTETH

River Mersey

Ropewalks and around p.60.
This former warehouse and factory district roughly between Bold Street and Duke Street is at the heart of Liverpool's regenerating city centre, particularly in the hip bars and restaurants of the Baltic Triangle.

Waterfront p.34.
The Royal Liver Building is one of Liverpool's great landmarks, while the iconic Albert Dock is now home to several museums including the Tate Liverpool. Though it's no longer a working dockland, this area remains the heart of Liverpool.

DINGLE

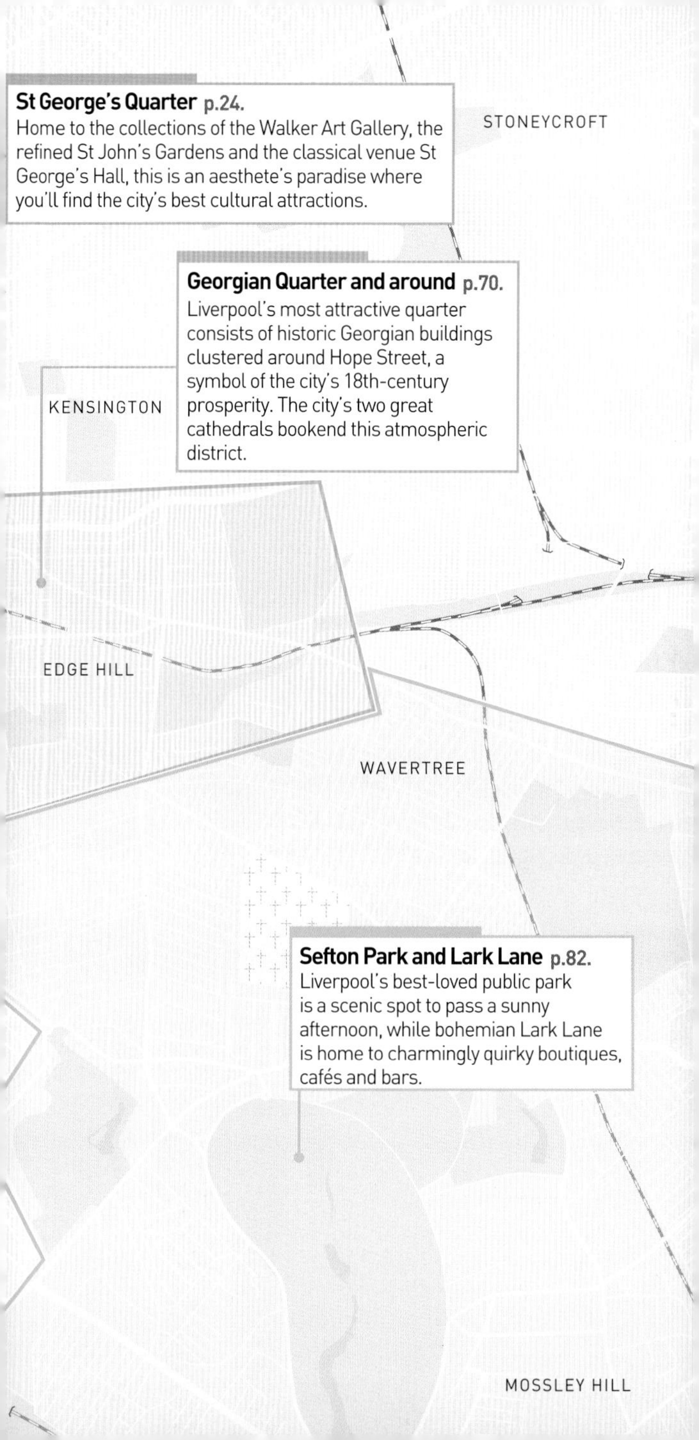

STONEYCROFT

St George's Quarter p.24.
Home to the collections of the Walker Art Gallery, the refined St John's Gardens and the classical venue St George's Hall, this is an aesthete's paradise where you'll find the city's best cultural attractions.

Georgian Quarter and around p.70.
Liverpool's most attractive quarter consists of historic Georgian buildings clustered around Hope Street, a symbol of the city's 18th-century prosperity. The city's two great cathedrals bookend this atmospheric district.

KENSINGTON

EDGE HILL

WAVERTREE

Sefton Park and Lark Lane p.82.
Liverpool's best-loved public park is a scenic spot to pass a sunny afternoon, while bohemian Lark Lane is home to charmingly quirky boutiques, cafés and bars.

MOSSLEY HILL

15

Things not to miss

It's not possible to see everything that Liverpool has to offer in one trip – and we don't suggest you try. What follows is a selective taste of the city's highlights, from museums to model villages.

> Bold Street
See page 61
Liverpool's greatest shopping street, lined with fantastic restaurants, bars and boutiques, is at the heart of the rejuvenated Ropewalks district.

< Crosby Beach
See page 99
What had once been a picturesque but unremarkable sandy beach was transformed into an eerily beautiful art installation with the unveiling of Antony Gormley's Another Place statues.

∨ Albert Dock
See page 34
Once at the vanguard of Liverpool's position as a major port, today the rejuvenated dock houses several museums and a range of fantastic restaurants, cafés, shops and bars.

< Liverpool Cathedral
See page 70
Britain's largest cathedral (and the fifth largest in the world) is a mightily impressive work of neo-Gothic architecture, featuring modern art by Tracey Emin.

∨ The Ferry Across the Mersey
See page 39
Immortalized in song by Gerry & The Pacemakers, this remains the way to cross from Liverpool to the Wirral in style.

< **Anfield and Goodison Park**
See pages 96 and 97
Football rivals music as Liverpool's greatest asset, and the homes of Liverpool and Everton (pictured) are the best places to catch a game.

∨ **Port Sunlight**
See page 101
Home to an amazing 900 listed buildings, the model village of Port Sunlight was built to house the workers of the Lever Brothers soap company.

∧ Royal Liver Building
See page 43

The most iconic of Liverpool's Three Graces, the Royal Liver Building opened to the public for the first time in 2019, its history brought to life by the immersive RLB360 audiovisual exhibit.

< Walker Art Gallery
See page 24

The city's finest art gallery contains works by the likes of Cézanne, Monet and David Hockney, as well as the superb animal artworks of local artist George Stubbs.

∧ **Magical Mystery Tour**
See page 35
The Beatles fans will love this whistle-stop tour of the band's former haunts, including their childhood homes, Strawberry Field and Penny Lane.

∨ **Metropolitan Cathedral**
See page 74
This space-age 1960s structure is one of Liverpool's most recognizable buildings, and the heart of the city's Roman Catholic population.

∧ Museum of Liverpool
See page 38
The finest among a bevy of top-quality museums is this space-age building, which resembles a vacuum cleaner attachment and contains exhibits on Liverpool's rich and colourful history.

< Cavern Club
See page 50
Legendary nightclub where The Beatles cut their teeth in their early career. Having closed and reopened repeatedly in the decades since, it remains an atmospheric place to catch a live band.

< **Tate Liverpool**
See page 34
Housed in the rejuvenated
Albert Dock, this world-class
art museum showcases works
from the Tate collection, including
pieces by Mark Rothko, Louise
Bourgeois and Claes Oldenburg.

∨ **Sefton Park**
See page 82
Liverpool's loveliest park, with its
boating lake, obelisk and shaded
grottoes, offers a welcome refuge
from the bustle of the city.

THINGS NOT TO MISS

Day One in Liverpool

St George's Quarter. See page 24. Begin your tour of Liverpool by exploring the collections of the Walker Art Gallery.

World Museum. See page 25. Learn all about Egyptian mummies and dinosaurs. A must for those interested in archaeology, anthropology and the natural world.

Bold Street. See page 61. Head southeast to the regenerated Ropewalks district and browse the boutiques of Liverpool's finest shopping street.

Lunch. See page 66. Enjoy lunch at Maray. Indulge in a variety of flavours mostly from the Mediterranean and the Middle East.

Walker Art Gallery

St Luke's Bombed Out Church. See page 63. Found at the end of Bold Street, stop at this atmospheric building which lost its roof to the carnage of the Liverpool Blitz.

Metropolitan Cathedral. See page 74. Northeast of St Luke's lies an altogether more modern church, whose space-age exterior encloses a beautiful stained-glass atrium.

The Williamson Tunnels. See page 75. Next head for one of Liverpool's most enduring mysteries. The tunnels are a cavern of subterranean passageways and rooms, built for enigmatic purposes by a wealthy industrialist.

Liverpool Cathedral. See page 70. Walk down the stately Hope Street to the city's other great church. A looming hulk of red sandstone, this combines traditional architecture with a Tracey Emin art installation.

Chinatown. See page 64. Announced by a magnificent arch, this is Europe's oldest Chinatown.

Dinner. See page 66. End your day with a delicious Szechuan dinner at Mr Chilli.

Metropolitan Cathedral

Chinatown

Day Two in Liverpool

Albert Dock. See page 34. Begin your second day on the waterfront, at this reincarnated part of the city.

The Beatles Story. See page 35. Discover more about Liverpool's most famous sons.

Tate Liverpool. See page 34. Continue walking around the dock until you reach the world-class museum where permanent galleries and guest installations showcase the work of the world's most famous artists.

Merseyside Maritime Museum. See page 38. End your time on the waterfront where exhibits tell the story of Merseyside's seafaring past – including the dark chapter of slavery.

 Lunch. See page 46. Enjoy lunch with a view at Panoramic 34. Think seasonal British produce at its very best.

Anfield. See page 96. Jump in a cab to and take a tour of one of the world's most famous football grounds.

Bluecoat building. See page 61. Heading back to town, visit a stunning a former school which is now one of the city's most vibrant arts centres.

Mathew Street. See page 26. Spend the evening at the place in Liverpool most associated with The Beatles.

 Dinner. See page 55. Enjoy a meal at Bistro Pierre. Think rustic French country cuisine.

Venue. See page 50. After dinner, head to the legendary Cavern Club and catch a show.

The Beatles Story

Anfield

Bluecoat building

A Beatles Itinerary

Alongside football, The Beatles are the biggest draw for visitors to Liverpool, and a tour of the sights associated with the band is a great way to spend a day.

20 Forthlin Road. See page 90. Begin your Beatles tour at the childhood home of Paul McCartney. Now a National Trust property, the house has been restored to be exactly as it was when Paul's family lived here.

Mendips. See page 89. Explore the childhood home of John Lennon, also restored by the National Trust to look as Lennon would've known it.

Strawberry Field. See page 89. Close to Mendips is a former orphanage which was the inspiration for a great Beatles song. It opened to the public for the first time in 2019.

Penny Lane. See page 88. A short way west of Strawberry Fields is the street which inspired McCartney's legendary song of the same name. Keep an eye out for the barbers mentioned in the first verse.

Magical Beatles Museum. See page 50. Back in town, wrap up your tour with a visit to this waterfront spot and learn more about the Fab Four.

Dinner. See page 55. Enjoy a down-to-earth bistro dinner at The Cavern Restaurant.

Venue. See page 50. Enjoy a tribute band at the famous live music venue Cavern Club.

20 Forthlin Road

Penny Lane

Cavern Club display

Budget/Free Liverpool

Thanks to a plethora of free museums and galleries, enjoying Liverpool doesn't have to cost the earth – or even anything at all.

Tate Liverpool. See page 34. One of the country's finest art galleries, where you can marvel at the works of Kandinsky, Warhol and Dalí – all for free.

Museum of Liverpool. See page 38. Down the waterfront is this futuristic spot where exhibits tell the story of the city from its ancient past to the vibrant present.

Crosby Beach. See page 99. Take the quick train ride up the coast where Antony Gormely's Another Place statues gaze blankly out to sea – a stunning sight.

Lark Lane. See page 86. Back in town, trundle down this bohemian street. Spend an hour or two browsing the street's quirky boutiques and cafés.

 Lunch. See page 92. Enjoy a cheap, delicious Middle Eastern lunch at Hafla Hafla.

Sefton Park. See page 82. See out the afternoon by walking along shaded paths to classical fountains, meadows and the beautiful Palm House.

Dinner. See page 81. Enjoy a great-value Mediterranean meal at Kimos Café.

Baltic Triangle. See page 64. After finishing your meal, check out the buzzing bars of the Baltic Triangle area.

Tate Liverpool

Crosby Beach

Live music at Baltic Market

PLACES

A stunning view of the Liver Building

St George's Quarter

The area immediately to the northwest of Lime Street Station, St George's Quarter is home to some of Liverpool's most refined Victorian buildings and premier cultural institutions. Part of Liverpool's UNESCO-listed historic core, this is where you'll find the magnificent Central Library, the city's finest art gallery and a superb natural history and anthropology museum, along with several theatres and events venues.

St George's Hall

MAP P.26
St George's Place, off Lime St, L1. Metro: Lime Street. http://stgeorgeshallliverpool. co.uk. Mon–Sat 9.30am–5pm. Free.

Emerging from Lime Street Station, you can't miss St George's Hall, one of Britain's finest Greek Revival buildings and a testament to the wealth generated from transatlantic trade. Now primarily an exhibition and events venue, but once Liverpool's premier concert hall and crown court, its vaulted Great Hall features a floor tiled with thirty thousand precious Minton tiles (usually covered over, but open for a week or two in Aug), while the Willis organ is the third largest in Europe. You can take a self-guided tour, or call for details of the guided tours.

Walker Art Gallery

MAP P.26
William Brown St, L3. Metro: Lime Street. http://liverpoolmuseums.org.uk/walker. Tues–Sun 10am–4pm. Free.

Liverpool's Walker Art Gallery houses one of the country's best provincial art collections. The city's explosive economic growth in the eighteenth and nineteenth centuries, a time when British painting began to blossom, is illustrated by such luminaries as native Liverpudlian George Stubbs, England's greatest animal painter. Impressionists and Post-Impressionists, including Degas, Sickert, Cézanne and Monet, take the collection into more modern times and tastes, before the final round of galleries of contemporary British art. Paul Nash, Lucian Freud, Ben Nicholson, David Hockney and John Hoyland all have work here, much of it first displayed in the Walker's biennial John Moores Exhibition.

Although the paintings are up on the first floor, don't miss the ground-floor with its Sculpture gallery, excellent Big Art for Little Artists gallery (aimed at young children), and the Decorative Art gallery, which displays changing exhibits from a large applied arts collection – glassware, ceramics, fabrics, precious metals and furniture – largely retrieved from the homes of the city's early industrial businessmen.

Central Library

MAP P.26
William Brown St, L3. Metro: Lime Street. http://liverpool.gov.uk/libraries/find-a-library/central-library. Mon–Fri 9am–8pm, Sat 9am–5pm. Free.

Next to the Walker Gallery, the city's spectacular Central Library had a three-year, £50 million facelift back in 2013. Approached via a "Literary Pavement" celebrating the city's considerable contribution to the written word, it centres on a stunning atrium crowned by an elliptical dome made of around 150 pieces of glass. Don't miss the beautiful circular Picton Reading

Room, which is among the most beautiful of its kind anywhere – the walls are lined with rich, dark wood shelving packed from floor to ceiling with books, and the room is circled around a monumental wooden pillar topped with a vast flower-shaped lamp, symbolising the illumination of knowledge (this was also the first British library to have fully electrified lighting). All the while, marble busts of Hugh Frederick Hornby and James Picton, for whom the library buildings are named, watch on sternly. In the Oak Room, you can't miss the huge glass-cased copy of John James Audubon's huge *Birds of America*, a seminal work of 19th-century naturalism illustrated by beautiful life-size prints. Six of the species included, among them the passenger pigeon and Labrador duck, are now sadly extinct.

Liverpool World Museum

MAP P.26

William Brown St, L3. Metro: Lime Street. http://liverpoolmuseums.org.uk/wml. Tues–Sun 10am–4pm. Free.

Liverpool's World Museum is a big draw for anyone interested in archaeology, anthropology and the natural world, with exhibits that will enthral kids and adults alike from Ancient Egyptian mummies to awesome dinosaur skeletons. The dramatic six-storey atrium provides access to an eclectic series of themed exhibits of broad appeal – from natural history to ethnography, insects to antiquities, and dinosaurs to space rockets. Excellent sections for children include the Bug House – where real specimens are displayed alongside spooky plus-sized models – and the Planetarium, where video technology brings to life the mysteries of the cosmos, including the tantalizing possibility of alien life. The planetarium and theatre have daily shows, with times posted at the information desk. The museum also has a vibrant programme of temporary exhibitions on subjects as diverse as ancient gods and AI.

St John's Gardens

MAP P.26

St George's Place, L1. Metro: Lime Street. http://liverpool.gov.uk/leisure-parks-and-events. Daily 24hr. Free.

Central Library

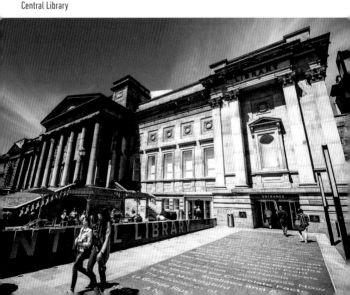

The atrium at Liverpool World Museum

St George's Hall, the Central Library and the World Museum are clustered around the elegant

St John's Gardens, a lovely area of lawns, flowerbeds and pathways dotted with sculptures of luminaries from various fields: William Gladstone, the 19th-century Liberal prime minister who was born on Rodney Street in Liverpool; Scottish shipping magnate Alexander Balfour; and James Nugent, a Catholic priest who set up several orphanages and schools for disadvantaged children. One of very few green spaces within the centre of Liverpool, the gardens are a peaceful sanctuary from the bustle of the city centre, and a lovely spot to sit down on a bench and have a breather in between trudging around museums and galleries.

Liverpool Empire

MAP P.26

Lime St, L1. Metro: Lime Street. http:// liverpooltheatres.com.

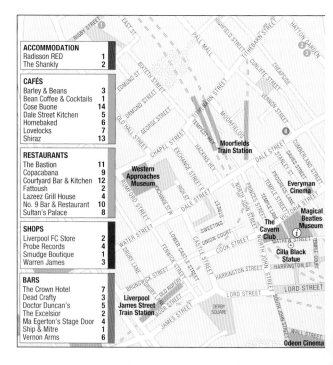

ACCOMMODATION

| Radisson RED | 1 |
| The Shankly | 2 |

CAFÉS

Barley & Beans	3
Bean Coffee & Cocktails	1
Cose Buone	14
Dale Street Kitchen	5
Homebaked	6
Lovelocks	7
Shiraz	13

RESTAURANTS

The Bastion	11
Copacabana	9
Courtyard Bar & Kitchen	12
Fattoush	2
Lazeez Grill House	4
No. 9 Bar & Restaurant	10
Sultan's Palace	8

SHOPS

Liverpool FC Store	2
Probe Records	4
Smudge Boutique	1
Warren James	3

BARS

The Crown Hotel	7
Dead Crafty	3
Doctor Duncan's	5
The Excelsior	2
Ma Egerton's Stage Door	4
Ship & Mitre	1
Vernon Arms	6

Opened in 1925, the legendary Empire remains Liverpool's largest theatre and the largest two-tier auditorium in Britain, seating 2,348 people. Built in a Neoclassical style, with elephant pillars and a regal red-and-gold colour scheme, the venue has hosted a wide array of performers over the last century, from music hall and variety acts in the early years to The Beatles in the early Sixties and Kate Bush, Elton John and Kylie Minogue in the years since. Today the agenda is similarly diverse, with international touring comedians and bands, tribute acts and ballet troupes all regularly gracing the stage. Like any old theatre worth its salt, the Empire has its share of resident ghosts. Many employees have reported seeing a little girl in Victorian dress in the Stalls bar, being dragged away by a man with dark eyes. Les the Painter, meanwhile, is apparently a former employee who just couldn't let his former place of work go and is often seen roaming the corridors.

Liverpool Playhouse Theatre

MAP P.26

Williamson Square, L1. Bus: Mount Pleasant. http://everymanplayhouse.com.

The sister theatre to the Everyman, the Playhouse stages bold productions of great plays in the three-tier main house and new plays in the seventy-seat Studio. Opening in 1866, it was originally a music hall before repurposing as a repertory theatre in 1911; the Playhouse's association with emerging talent and traditional work abides to this day. Future megastars who cut their teeth here in times gone by include Noël Coward, Anthony Hopkins and Rex Harrison. Architecturally, the theatre reflects both its heritage

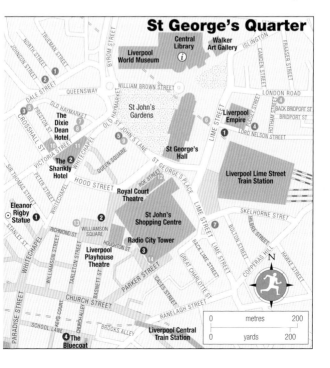

Radio City Tower

in the second half of the 20th century – a young Judi Dench made her first stage appearance here in 1957 as Ophelia in Hamlet, while Richard Burton and Fred Astaire are among the other legendary performers to tread the Royal Court's boards. This is yet another Liverpool location of tangential interest to Beatles fans, as the previous theatre on the site, Cooke's Royal Amphitheatre of Arts, played host to circus performer Pablo Fanque, immortalized in the Sgt Pepper song '*Being for the Benefit of Mr Kite*'.

Radio City Tower

MAP P.26
1 Houghton St, L1. Metro: Lime Street. http://stjohnsbeacon.co.uk. Daily 10am–5.15pm. Charge.
Looming above the St John's Shopping Centre is the 452ft-tall Radio City Tower, also known as St John's Beacon. Opened in 1969, it was Liverpool's tallest building (overtaking the Anglican Cathedral) for 39 years before the West Tower opened on the waterfront in 2008. The very height of Space Race cool when it opened, complete with a modish revolving restaurant, the building has rather fallen in favour in the decades since, although a welcome renovation in 1999 saw the then-derelict tower repurposed as the headquarters of local radio station Radio City 96.7. Today the former restaurant floor houses the radio studios (and no longer revolves), though visitors can buy refreshments at what is tantalisingly described as "the best-value vending machine in Liverpool." If that isn't enough to tempt you in, the 394ft viewing platform offers genuinely superb views over the city and beyond; on a clear day (admittedly not guaranteed), it is possible to see as far as Blackpool to the north and Snowdonia to the southwest.

and its forward-facing ethos: the original building has a pleasingly proportioned Neoclassical facade, topped with two gilded domes, while the newer section, to the left as you face the building, is a modern glass assemblage of stacked cylinders. The theatre's diverse line-up reflects a continuing commitment to emerging talent and forward-facing theatre, putting on plays by local writers alongside acclaimed touring productions from the National Theatre and further afield.

Royal Court Theatre

MAP P.26
Roe St, L1. Metro: Lime Street. http://liverpoolsroyalcourt.com.
Contrasting with Liverpool's grand Victorian theatres is this boxy, redbrick Art Deco construction dating from 1938. The Royal Court survived the devastation of the Blitz to see a number of stars grace its stage

Shops

Liverpool FC Store

MAP P.26

Williamson Square, L1. Metro: Liverpool
Central or Moorfields. http://liverpoolfc.
com. Mon–Sat 9am–5.30pm, Sun
10am–4pm.

If your idea of the perfect gift or
souvenir is a shirt or scarf from a
city's biggest football team, head
to this official Liverpool FC store
where you're guaranteed to find
authentic merchandise. With the
team having won their first ever
Premier League title in 2020, a
shirt of recent vintage might prove
to be a tidy investment. Other
outlets at Liverpool ONE (see page
61) and Anfield Stadium (see
page 96).

Probe Records

MAP P.26

1 The Bluecoat, School Ln, L1. Metro:
Liverpool Central or Moorfields. www.
probe-records.uk. Mon–Sat 10am–6pm,
Sun 12.30–4.30pm.

There are some great finds to be
had at this long-standing record
shop, open for more than fifty years

Liverpool FC Store

and now situated in the gorgeous
Bluecoat building. Well worth a
look, whether you're after some rare
vinyl or a classic British rock album
– The Beatles, anyone?

Smudge Boutique

MAP P.26

Unit 7, Metquarter Shopping Centre, L1.
Metro: Liverpool Central or Moorfields.
http://smudgeboutique.com. Mon–Sat
10am–6pm, Sun 11am–4pm.

This popular women's fashion
boutique sells wide-ranging
offerings by UK and international
designers, including luxury
Bamboa swimwear, sheepskin
slippers from Emu Australia,
jewellery by Envy, and casual wear
by Sofie Schnoor.

Warren James

MAP P.26

Lower Level, St John's Shopping Centre,
L1. Metro: Liverpool Central or Moorfields.
http://warrenjames.co.uk. Mon–Sat
9.15am–5.30pm, Sun 11am–5pm.

This jewellery chain now has
outlets across the UK, but it started
life not far from Liverpool, 30
miles to the east in Stockport. A
necklace, ring or set of earrings

Liverpool FC

makes the perfect gift or souvenir of your stay.

Restaurants

The Bastion

MAP P.26

60 Victoria St, L1. Metro: Lime St or Moorfields. http://shanklyhotel.com. Daily 11am–11pm.

Those with an interest in football may like the unique decor of *The Bastion* – though Everton fans might want to give it a miss. The visage of legendary Liverpool manager Bill Shankly smiles down at you from the walls and up at you from the menus at this restaurant, housed in the *Shankly Hotel*, which follows a similar theme. The Chesterfield furnishings and padded armchairs make a comfy setting for superb afternoon tea and other traditional British offerings like slow braised lamb shoulder and seared duck breast. £££

Copacabana

MAP P.26

1 St John's House, L1. Metro: Lime St or Moorfields. http://copacabanaliverpool. co.uk. Sun–Thurs noon–10pm, Fri–Sat until 11pm.

The 'Brazilian steakhouse' restaurant format is very en vogue across the United Kingdom these days, with Liverpool no exception – and this is one of the city's finest examples. Food is served *rodizio* style, which means that for a fixed price you eat as much as you like from a selection of grilled meats including flank steak, ribs, parmesan pork and chicken hearts – the attentive waiting staff will keep replenishing your plate until you signal that you can go on no longer. ££–£££

Courtyard Bar & Kitchen

MAP P.26

89 Roe St, L1. Metro: Lime Street. http://courtyardbk.co.uk. Mon–Thurs 3pm–midnight, Fri–Sat until 2am.

Boasting unrivalled views of St George's Hall through wall-length windows, the *Courtyard Bar & Kitchen* is a stylish space with racing green leather banquettes, hanging plants and exposed redbrick walls. The menu is a nicely diverse affair, with some hearty British classics like slow-stewed lamb and chicken pot pie alongside more exotic offerings like red lentil masala. There's also a good range of cocktails, wines and beers, including local cask ales. ££–£££

Fattoush

MAP P.26

23 Hatton Garden, L3. Metro: Moorfields. http://fattoushliverpool.com. Daily 11am–11pm.

Liverpool's finest Lebanese restaurant is an atmospheric space, with a lovely *azulejo*-tiled counter and walls bearing photographs of Middle Eastern ruins and palaces. The food is superb; self-styled as 'Lebanese-Mediterranean', the menu offers a lovely selection of meze dishes, juicy BBQ meats and spit-roasted shawarmas, all at great prices. Just make sure you leave room to try a *baklava* or milk pudding for dessert. £

Lazeez Grill House

MAP P.26

34–36 London Rd, L1. Metro: Lime Street. 0774 706 5059. Daily noon–9pm.

Don't let the bright logo and oversized meal photos of the exterior fool you – this is far more than a cheap kebab takeaway. Inside it's a pleasant if unspectacular place for a sit-down meal, but the star attraction is the Kurdish cuisine. Mountains of aromatic rice, topped with beautifully marinated lamb or tender chicken wings, accompanied by fresh, zingy salads or grilled vegetables – the portions are huge and the food delicious. Go for the *quozy* – a superb value combination of a meat dish, rice, stew and potato side. £

The Crown Hotel

No. 9 Bar & Restaurant

MAP P.26

67 Victoria St, L1. Metro: Moorfields. http://dixiedeanhotel.co.uk. Mon–Sat noon–9.30pm, Sun until 8.30pm.

Part of the *Dixie Dean Hotel*, another Liverpool property dedicated to a football legend (this time Everton forward Dixie Dean), this restaurant is quite the eyeful – redbrick walls and wooden beams jostle for space with blue velvet chairs, leather padded bars and gilded baroque mirrors – but somehow it all works. The food is superb: a mostly British menu includes Conwy crab and Bowland lamb and is complemented by Italian offerings like wild mushroom pappardelle and cauliflower risotto. ££–£££

Sultan's Palace

MAP P.26

75–77 Victoria St, L1. Metro: Lime St or Moorfields. http://sultans-palace.co.uk. Tues–Thurs & Sun 5–10pm, Fri–Sat until 10.30pm.

'Palatial' might be pushing it, but this celebrated city centre Indian restaurant is certainly elegant, with its high ceilings, wall niches and grand arches. Happily, the food is good enough to match, with a hearty menu of meaty, rich Mughal curries from the north of India. Tandoori dishes, rubbed with dry spices and cooked in a clay oven, are a particular speciality – try the mixed grill or the lamb chops. ££

Bars

The Crown Hotel

MAP P.26

43 Lime St, L1. Metro: Lime Street. www.thecrownliverpool.co.uk. Mon–Sat 9am–10pm, Sun 10am–10pm.

Despite the name, this is a pub, not a hotel, and a beauty of a pub it is too. Built in 1905, it has an Art Nouveau look, particularly in the eye-catching signage. Inside, it's an elegant space with tiled floors and high, ornately stuccoed ceilings – the perfect place to kill some time before a train from Lime St.

Dead Crafty

MAP P.26

92 Dale St, L2. Metro: Moorfields. http://www.deadcraftybeercompany.com. Mon–Thurs 3–11pm, Fri–Sat noon–midnight, Sun noon–11pm.

The craft beer wave has not passed Liverpool by, and there is a growing number of bars in town specializing in artisanal brews from the UK and across the world. This is one of the best, with 20 taps serving an ever-changing roster of beers, a friendly welcome, and the standard chipboard-and-exposed brick aesthetic which seems to be obligatory in such places.

Doctor Duncan's

MAP P.26

St John's Ln, Queens Square, L1. Metro: Lime Street. www.doctorduncansliverpool. com. Daily noon–11pm.

If real ale is your thing, get yourself down to *Doctor Duncan's*, which at the latest count was welcoming a whopping 700 guest beers per year and has won awards for the quality of its cask beer. Even if the thought of drinking room-temperature beer makes you want to run for the hills, it's still a lovely spot, with its leather armchairs, ornate columns and tiled walls.

The Excelsior

MAP P.26

121–123 Dale St, L2. Metro: Moorfields. http://excelsiorliverpool.co.uk. Mon–Thurs & Sun noon–10.30pm, Fri noon–11pm, Sat 11am–11pm.

Ship & Mitre

Adjacent to the *Ship & Mitre*, this is another traditional English pub where it's very easy to nestle in to a corner sofa with a beer or glass of wine and watch the hours melt away. There's occasional live music, and a good line in pies and other pub grub dishes.

Ma Egerton's Stage Door

MAP P.26

9 Pudsey St, L1. Metro: Lime Street. http:// maegertons.com. Mon–Sat 11am–midnight, Sun noon–11pm.

Next door to the Empire Theatre, this *grand dame* of Liverpool watering holes dates back all the way to 1869, and has accumulated enough theatrical heritage to fill a book – among the famous patrons is Harry Houdini, said to have entertained fellow drinkers with an impromptu performance in 1914. Today the pub has been lovingly refurbished in the Victorian style, and is one of the most atmospheric spots in town for a pre- or post-theatre drink.

Ship & Mitre

MAP P.26

133 Dale St, L2. Metro: Moorfields. http:// theshipandmitre.com. Daily 11am–11pm, Fri–Sat until midnight.

Perfectly placed for a quick pint after an afternoon tramping around the World Museum, the *Ship & Mitre* is a boozer with iconic status in Liverpool, and has been named by the *Guardian* as one of the country's best pubs. There's a huge selection of real ales on tap, and the rather bland exterior hides some lovely interior period features, like stained glass windows and wrought-iron lanterns.

Vernon Arms

MAP P.26

69 Dale St, L2. Metro: Moorfields. www. facebook.com/TheVernonArmsL2. Daily noon–11pm.

No trip to Liverpool, or any British city for that matter, is complete without a trip to a traditional pub – and this boozer, with its gloomy lighting, wine-red Chesterfield sofas, and a good selection of ales on tap, certainly fits in that category.

Cafés

Barley & Beans

17 Hatton Gardens, L3. Metro: Moorfields. http://barleyandbeans.co.uk. Mon–Thurs 9.30am–8pm, Fri–Sun until 9pm.

The 'freak shakes' at this trendy café – loaded with ice cream, marshmallows and candy floss – are enough to induce a heart attack at twenty paces, while the mac and cheese fries, cheeseburgers and pancakes aren't much healthier. Delicious, though. ££

Bean Coffee & Cocktails

3 St Paul's Square, L3. Bus: Edmund St. http://beancoffee.co.uk. Mon–Thurs 7am–4pm, Fri 7.30am–8pm.

With a few outlets across the city, this trendy café does superb coffee and delicious home-made baguettes and pizzas. It also briefly turns into a bar on Friday evenings, with 2-for-1 deals on beer and wine between 4.30–5.30pm, and a decent selection of cocktails. £

Cose Buone

Unit 100 St John's Market, L3. Metro: Moorfields. http://facebook.com/cosebuoneliverpool. Mon–Fri 10am–5pm, Sat until 5.30pm.

This tiny Sicilian-run place is always popular for its espresso-based coffees and Italian food – pick up a couple of *arancini* or a slice of cassata cake for a quick snack, or opt for a more substantial pizza or calzone. The meal deals are good value. £

Dale Street Kitchen

90 Dale St, L2. Metro: Moorfields. http://dalestkitchen.co.uk. Daily 8am–5pm.

Lovely café with wooden floors, tiled walls, and vintage photographs of Liverpool past adorning the wall. The menu offers a lovely balance of international offerings, from traditional English breakfasts to Middle Eastern plates of falafel, hummus and roasted peppers. It's all great, and there's superb coffee to match. ££

Homebaked

St George's Hall, L1. Metro: Lime Street. www.stgeorgeshallliverpool.co.uk. Tues–Sat 9am–4pm.

This cosy spot inside St. George's Hall, an offshoot of a local Anfield institution, is beloved for its pies, with favourite fillings including chicken and veg, scouse, chicken curry, and mushroom and brandy. Community-owned, the company puts profits into local initiatives. £

Lovelocks

Unit 6 Old Haymarket, L1. Metro: Lime Street or Moorfields. http://lovelocks.coffee. Mon–Fri 8am–4pm, Sat 10am–4pm.

The cosy name is matched by the atmosphere at this charming café within sight of St John's Gardens and St George's Hall. There's a build-your-own menu of healthy granola and toast options, some lovely bagels, soups and stews, and top coffee to boot. £

Shiraz Palace

45 Ranelagh Street, L1. Metro: Lime Street. 0151 707 7700. Daily 9.30am–11pm, Fri–Sat until midnight.

There's not much that's Iranian about *Shiraz's* huge English breakfasts (which are justifiably popular), although it comes more into line with its name later in the day, with a delicious selection of Persian lamb dishes – alongside pizzas, Greek salads and cottage pie. More a café than a restaurant, it's a pleasant spot to sit with a coffee for a while and enjoy the atmosphere. Becomes a lively cocktail bar later in the day. £

Waterfront

Nowhere encapsulates Liverpool's recent rebirth like its iconic Waterfront. Representing the vast wealth of the Industrial Age are the so-called Three Graces – namely the Port of Liverpool Building (1907), Cunard Building (1913) and, most prominently, the 322ft-high Royal Liver Building (1910), topped by the "Liver Birds", which have become the symbol of the city (see page 43). As the waterfront has developed in the last decade or so, it has sprouted a number of attractions, including Tate Liverpool, the excellent Merseyside Maritime Museum, The Beatles Story, the impressive Museum of Liverpool and the marvellous Open Eye gallery. Five minutes' walk south of Pier Head, from where departs the famous *Ferry Across the Mersey* (see page 39) is Albert Dock, built in 1846 when Liverpool's port was a world leader. Its decline began at the beginning of the twentieth century, as the new deep-draught ships were unable to berth here, and the dock last saw service in 1972. A decade later the site was given a refit, and it is now one of the city's most popular areas, full of attractions, bars and restaurants.

Royal Albert Dock

MAP P.36
Albert Dock, L3. Bus: Strand St.
Boasting the largest collection of Grade I-listed buildings in the country, the Royal Albert Dock encapsulates the regeneration of Liverpool and the Waterfront better than anywhere else. It was here, in the nineteenth century, that many of the valuable tobacco, sugar, silk, tea and other commodities that passed through Liverpool's port were stored; in particular, the dock dominated the city's lucrative trade with the Far East. By the early twentieth century, however, things had slowed down significantly, and in 1972 the dock was closed and allowed to fill with silt and sewage from the River Mersey. The 1980s saw a drive to redevelop the docks, and in 1988 Albert Dock was reopened along the unveiling of the new jewel in its crown, the Tate Liverpool.

Tate Liverpool

MAP P.36
Albert Dock, L3. Bus: Strand St. http:// tate.org.uk/visit/tate-liverpool. Daily 10am–5.50pm. Free.
The country's national collection of modern art for the north, Tate Liverpool holds popular retrospectives of artists such as Mondrian, Dalí, Magritte and Calder, along with an ever-changing display from its vast collection, and temporary exhibitions of artists of international standing. There's also a full programme of events, talks and tours. The large ground floor exhibition room, its smooth flagstones and vast cylindrical pillars representing the gallery at its most warehouse-like, is one of

the venues for staging international guest exhibits; the other is on the top floor. In between, artworks in the galleries are arranged according to 'constellations', with each star a different artist, related to their neighbour in terms of style or influence. This neat exhibition technique ensures a wide range of pieces can be displayed in a coherent order, while allowing visitors to discover new artists based on their existing preferences. Keep an eye out (you can hardly miss it) for the *Liverpool Mountain*, an eye-catching installation just outside the Tate by Ugo Rondinone. Created in 2018, it consists of rainbow-coloured blocks stacked on top of one another in a top-heavy way which seems to defy gravity. Seven similar mountains, also by Rondinone, can be found brightening up the Mojave Desert outside Las Vegas.

Liverpool's premier Beatles museum offers a good overview of the Fab Four which will be particularly enlightening for those coming in with only a superficial knowledge of the band. Recreations of the *Cavern Club*, *The Casbah Coffee Club* (where John's first band The Quarrymen played their first gig), and John Lennon's famous white living room from the '*Imagine*' video paint a vivid picture of the band's story, as a group and individuals, from their earliest days together in Hamburg to their post-Beatles solo careers. Items of note include the famous military band suits worn by the band during the Sgt Pepper era; Lennon's glasses and his last piano, a stripped-down upright; Ringo's drum kit and various other instruments; and handwritten lyrics, drawings, and personal photography.

The Beatles Story

MAP P.36
Albert Dock, L3. Bus: Salthouse Quay.
http://beatlesstory.com. Daily Apr–Oct
10am–6pm, Nov–Mar 9am–7pm, some
weekends in summer until 8pm. Charge.

Magical Mystery Tour

MAP P.36
Albert Dock, L3. Bus: Strand St. http://
cavernclub.com/the-magical-mystery-
tour. Tours depart at 10am, 11am, 1pm
& 2pm.

View towards the Tate Liverpool, Royal Albert Dock

Waterfront

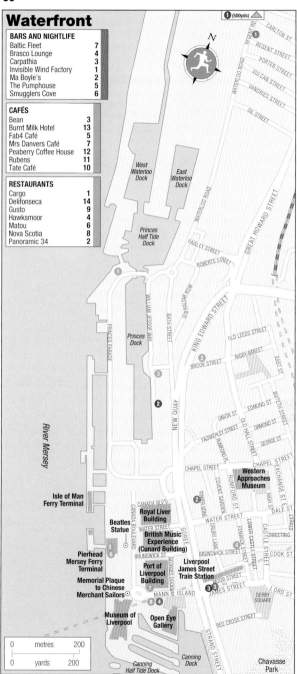

① (500yds)

BARS AND NIGHTLIFE

Baltic Fleet	7
Brasco Lounge	4
Carpathia	3
Invisible Wind Factory	1
Ma Boyle's	2
The Pumphouse	5
Smugglers Cove	6

CAFÉS

Bean	3
Burnt Milk Hotel	13
Fab4 Café	5
Mrs Danvers Café	7
Peaberry Coffee House	12
Rubens	11
Tate Café	10

RESTAURANTS

Cargo	1
Delifonseca	14
Gusto	9
Hawksmoor	4
Matou	6
Nova Scotia	8
Panoramic 34	2

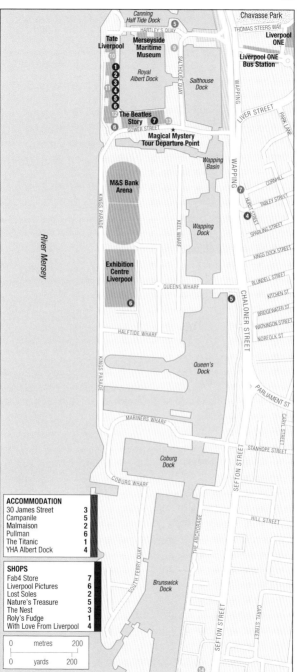

Chavasse Park

THOMAS STEERS WAY

Liverpool
ONE

Liverpool ONE
Bus Station

Canning
Half Tide Dock · 5

HARTLEY'S QUAY

Tate
Liverpool

10

Merseyside
Maritime
Museum

9

SALTHOUSE QUAY

1
2
3
4
11
5
6

Royal
Albert Dock

Salthouse
Dock

WAPPING

LIVER STREET

PARK LANE

12

6

The Beatles
Story

GOWER STREET

13

7

★ Magical Mystery
Tour Departure Point

CORNHILL

7

HURST STREET

4

TABLEY STREET

SPARLING STREET

M&S Bank
Arena

Wapping
Basin

WAPPING

KINGS PARADE

KEEL WHARF

Wapping
Dock

KINGS DOCK STREET

BLUNDELL STREET

KITCHEN ST

BRIDGEWATER ST

WATKINSON STREET

NORFOLK ST

CHALONER STREET

Exhibition
Centre
Liverpool

6

QUEENS WHARF

5

HALFTIDE WHARF

KINGS PARADE

Queen's
Dock

PARLIAMENT ST

River Mersey

MARINERS WHARF

STANHOPE STREET

CARYL STREET

SEFTON STREET

Coburg
Dock

COBURG WHARF

HILL STREET

SOUTH FERRY QUAY

THE ANCHORAGE

Brunswick
Dock

SEFTON STREET

CARYL STREET

14

ACCOMMODATION

30 James Street	3
Campanile	5
Malmaison	2
Pullman	6
The Titanic	1
YHA Albert Dock	4

SHOPS

Fab4 Store	7
Liverpool Pictures	6
Lost Soles	2
Nature's Treasure	5
The Nest	3
Roly's Fudge	1
With Love From Liverpool	4

0	metres	200
0	yards	200

Museum of Liverpool

The enjoyable Magical Mystery Tour departs from Gower St, on the southern edge of Albert Dock. On the face of it, it doesn't sound that interesting – a bus tour of suburban Liverpool, via the childhood homes and schools of The Beatles, plus a couple of other sites of interest. However, the enthusiasm and profound knowledge of the guides is what really makes the experience, bringing to life the ordinary streets and homes which proved to be such fertile creative ground for the Fab Four. All of the commentary is delivered while travelling inside the bus, interspersed with Beatles songs, and you disembark at selected points to have a closer look and take photos if you choose. These include George, John and Paul's childhood homes – the former privately owned, the latter two both National Trust Museums (Ringo's was off-limits due to construction at the time of research) – and the Penny Lane sign at the southern end of the road. The tour also stops outside Strawberry Field (see page 89), but doesn't go in – and they don't

mention that the gates you can photograph from outside are a replica. The original is in the garden – to see it, you have to come back another time pay to enter the site itself. The overpriced but pleasingly psychedelic bus to Strawberry Field also departs from Gower St, next to the Magical Mystery Tour bus.

Merseyside Maritime Museum

MAP P.36
Albert Dock, L3. Bus: Strand St. http://liverpoolmuseums.org.uk/maritime. Tues–Sun 10am–4pm. Free.

The Merseyside Maritime Museum fills one wing of the Dock; there's lots to see, even if some of the exhibits are looking a little tired. The basement houses Seized!, giving the lowdown on smuggling and revenue collection, along with Emigrants to a New World, an illuminating display detailing Liverpool's pivotal role as a springboard for more than nine million emigrants. Other galleries tell the story of the Battle of the Atlantic and of the three ill-fated liners – the *Titanic*, *Lusitania* and *Empress of Ireland*. The unmissable International Slavery Museum, on the third floor of the Maritime Museum, manages to be both challenging and chilling, as it tells dehumanizing stories of slavery while examining contemporary issues of equality, freedom and racial injustice.

Museum of Liverpool

MAP P.36
Pier Head, L3. Bus: Georges Pier Head. http://liverpoolmuseums.org.uk/mol. Tues–Sun 10am–4pm. Free.

Huge and flashy, in a show-stopping Danish-designed building, the brilliant Museum of Liverpool opened in 2011. Spread over three floors, the galleries play on Liverpool's historic status as the "second city of Empire", exploring the complex political and life histories that have unfolded in a community whose wealth and social fabric were built on international trade. Children will enjoy Little Liverpool, a gallery where they can design and build their own city, while anyone with any interest in popular culture will have an absolute ball at Wondrous Place, a memorabilia-rich celebration of sports and music.

Open Eye Gallery

MAP P.36
19 Mann Island, L3. Metro: James St. http://openeye.org.uk. Tues–Sun 10am–5pm. Free.

On the new Mann Island development just by the Museum of Liverpool sits the Open Eye Gallery, an obsidian-black crystal of a building that is a striking component of Liverpool's developing waterfront skyline. Dedicated to photography and related media, it hosts a revolving programme of international exhibitions and contains a permanent archive of around 1600 prints from the 1930s onwards. The gallery was originally established in 1977, in a different building in Liverpool's Whitechapel district; at the time it was one of the first dedicated photography galleries in the UK. The current modern building was built in 2011, and is the gallery's fourth home. The gallery is heavily involved in outreach community programmes and regularly exhibits work by local amateur and professional artists, while budding snappers can take a photography course here. Upcoming exhibitions in 2020 include The Dark Figure, a photo series by Amy Romer casting light on the phenomena of modern slavery, human trafficking and forced labour.

The Mersey Ferry

MAP P.36
Pier Head, George Parade, L3. Bus: Georges Pier Head. http://merseyferries.co.uk.

Hourly departures, daily 10am–4pm. Charge.

Though the tumult of shipping which once plied the River Mersey has gone, the Pier Head landing stage remains the embarkation point for the Mersey Ferry to Woodside (for Birkenhead) and Seacombe (Wallasey). Straightforward ferry shuttles operate during the morning and evening rush hours. At other times the boats run circular fifty-minute "river explorer" cruises (hourly: daily 10am–4pm, Sat & Sun until 6pm during summer), which include interesting commentary about the history of the ferries and life on both sides of the water, in Liverpool and the Wirral – punctuated, predictably enough, by slightly-too-loud blasts of Gerry and The Pacemakers' 1965 smash hit '*Ferry Cross the Mersey*'. For part of the year, usually during the winter, the route is plied *MV Snowdrop*, also known as the *Dazzle Ferry*, painted in psychedelic patterns by Peter Blake (who also designed the *Sgt Pepper's Lonely Hearts Club Band* cover). Explorer tickets could

Onboard the *MV Snowdrop*

The Beatles trail

Mathew Street, ten minutes' walk west of Lime Street Station, is now a little enclave of Beatles nostalgia, most of it bogus and typified by the Cavern Walks Shopping Centre, with a bronze statue of the boys in the atrium. The *Cavern Club* (see page 50), where the band was first spotted by Brian Epstein, saw 275 Beatles' gigs between 1961 and 1963; it closed in 1966 and was partly demolished in 1973, though a latter-day successor, the *Cavern Club* at 10 Mathew St, complete with souvenir shop, was rebuilt on the original site. The *Cavern Pub*, across the way, boasts a coiffed Lennon mannequin lounging against the wall and an exterior Wall of Fame highlighting the names of all the bands who appeared at the club between 1957 and 1973 as well as brass discs commemorating every Liverpool chart-topper since 1952 – the city has produced more UK No. 1 singles than any other. There's more Beatlemania at The Beatles Shop, 31 Mathew Street (facebook.com/OriginalBeatlesShop, see page54), which claims to have the largest range of Beatles gear in the world.

For a personal and social history, head to the Albert Dock for The Beatles Story (see page 35), which traces the band's rise from the early days to their disparate solo careers. Then it's on to the two houses where John Lennon and Paul McCartney grew up. Both 20 Forthlin Rd, home to the McCartney family from 1955 to 1964, and the rather more genteel Mendips, where Lennon lived with his Aunt Mimi and Uncle George between 1945 and 1963, are only accessible through prebooked National Trust minibus tours (see page 89 and see page 90), which run from both the city centre and Speke Hall, seven miles south (times for tours vary). The experience is disarmingly intimate, whether you're sitting in John Lennon's bedroom – which still has its original wallpaper – on a replica bed looking out, as he would have done, onto his front lawn, or simply entering Paul's tiny room and gazing at pictures

of his childhood; it'll be difficult not to be moved. Ever the bridesmaids, George and Ringo's childhood homes however have not been snapped up by the National Trust and turned into museums and instead remain privately owned.Tours will sometimes stop outside for fans to take a look.

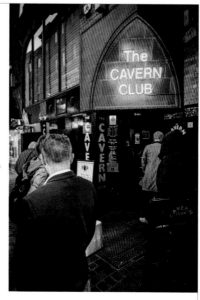

A number of guided Beatles tours are on offer in Liverpool, which take in the main sights relating to the band in more depth and with a more personal touch than you get on the big bus tours, which can carry dozens of visitors. The guides, for the most part, are fantastically passionate, friendly, and knowledgeable, and bring to life in vivid colour the places associated with the band – these tours are a better option for those who already have reasonably deep Beatles knowledge, who may find that the likes of the Magical Mystery Tour (see page 35) are going over things they already knew. As a disclaimer, though, a good rule of thumb is not to engage any of the tour guides in the hopes of getting a word in edgeways – they seem to operate in complete independence from the external world, and you feel that they would be talking about The Beatles even if there was no-one there to listen, which of course is part of their charm. Below are some recommended tour operators.

Mad Day Out Beatles Taxi Tours http://mad-dayouttaxitours. co.uk. The knowledgeable Ian Doyle leads visitors on a range of Beatles taxi trips, ranging from two to seven hours, in a Liverpool Hackney cab decked out in an eye-catching psychedelic design based on John Lennon's famous Rolls Royce Phantom V. In addition to the usual childhood homes, you'll visit the former home of manager Brian Epstein and the Percy Philips Studio where Beatles forerunners The Quarrymen recorded some early tracks. For the ultimate exclusive experience, book the Rocky VIP Tour (half-day/full day), which swaps the taxi for a beautiful vintage Rolls Royce Silver Shadow, hand-painted like Lennon's.

Phil Hughes http://tourliverpool.co.uk. Small (eight-seater) minibus tours run daily on demand with a Blue Badge guide well versed in The Beatles and life in Liverpool (4hr). These include city-centre pick-ups and drop-offs and refreshments en route.

Beatles Statue and Royal Liver Building

once be combined with a visit to the Spaceport space exploration visitor attraction at Seacombe, but this was closed in 2019 to make way for a new attraction, Eureka! Mersey (http://eurekamersey.org.uk), which opened in 2022 as another branch of the acclaimed children's museum in Halifax, West Yorkshire.

Beatles Statue

MAP P.36
Pier Head, L3, in front of the Mersey Ferry terminal. Bus: Georges Pier Head.
It seems remiss that so long should have passed before Liverpool's most famous sons were given pride of place in statuesque form (notwithstanding the rather naff efforts in Mathew St), but it wasn't until 2015 that this piece, by sculptor Andrew Edwards, appeared on Liverpool's waterfront. It coincided with the 50th anniversary of the boys' final Liverpool performance at the Empire Theatre, and shows them in their mid-Sixties morph, just before the suits and the moptops gave way to the Rubber Soul-era suede and shades. There are some Easter

eggs here for eagle-eyed visitors: the heel of Ringo's boot bears the inscription 'L8', in reference to the Liverpool postcode of his childhood and his 2008 album, while John is holding acorns in his right hand – a reference to the acorns he and Yoko sent to world leaders in 1969, as a symbol of peace.

British Music Experience

MAP P.36
Cunard Building, L3. Metro: James St. http://britishmusicexperience.com. Wed–Sun 10am–5pm. Charge.
Housed in the Cunard Building – one of the Liverpool waterfront's Three Graces – the British Music Experience is an essential stop if you have an interest in British culture and pop music, or if you have children in tow. The UK's premier pop and rock museum, it's a fun and interactive experience with loads of memorabilia from 1945 onwards on display, plus a hands-on instrument studio. The museum's dazzling collection of costumes includes David Bowie's technicolour stage outfits from the

Diamond Dogs tour, and other natty pieces worn by the likes of Freddy Mercury and Dusty Springfield. There are also guitars strummed by Noel Gallagher, Hank Marvin, Jimi Hendrix and Mani of the Stone Roses, alongside miscellany such as song lyrics handwritten by Adele.

Royal Liver Building

MAP P.36

Pier Head, L3. Bus: Cruise Terminal. http://rlb360.com. Daily 9am–4pm. Charge.

Foremost among Liverpool's iconic Three Graces stands the Liver Building, still the city's great symbol after more than 100 years. Built in 1911 as the headquarters of the Royal Liver Assurance bank, it was among the first buildings in the world to be built using reinforced concrete, and at the time of its construction was the tallest building not only in Liverpool but in Europe. It is now Liverpool's third tallest building, behind the West Tower, Radio City Tower, and the Anglican Cathedral, but Bella and Bertie, the famous liver birds who sit atop its twin clock towers, remain a visible landmark across much of the city. In September 2019, the Liver Building opened its doors to the public for the first time with the unveiling of RLB360, an immersive tour telling the story of the Liver Building from bottom to top. Beginning on the ground floor, an exhibition outlines the building's history before you are guided up to the tenth floor to take in magnificent panoramic views over Liverpool. You then climb up further, stopping inside the clock tower where a stunning video presentation is projected onto the inner walls. The tour ends with even more spectacular views from the 15th floor, right at the top of the tower. Tours last for 70 minutes and involve walking up narrow staircases, so this is not recommended for those with mobility issues. Children younger than seven are not allowed on the tour.

The liver bird

They may no longer crown Liverpool's tallest building, but the liver birds which sit atop the twin towers of the famous Liver Building remain a landmark visible across much of the city. The mythical bird has since become a symbol of Liverpool, adorning the city's crest and that of Liverpool Football club, but its exact origins are something of a mystery. The bird is often likened to a cormorant, a sea bird which is native to coastal England, although some historic references compare it with the spoonbill. Liverpool's ancient seal bears the image of a bird too generic to be given any certain taxonomic status. What is clear is that the idea of the distinct mythical creature of the liver bird only really took hold in the local imagination after the construction of the Liver Building in 1911. The creation of the two striking copper birds fuelled the creation of a modern legend of a mythical creature which once stalked the Liverpool shoreline, watching over the city. It's said that the Liver Building's two birds, nicknamed Bella and Bertie, fulfil that role to this day: Bella looking out to the ocean to protect the sailors, and Bertie looking inland over their families and the citizens of Liverpool. It's thought to be important that they face away from one another, as if they were to mate and fly away, the Mersey would burst its banks, leaving Liverpool in ruin.

Shops

Fab4 Store

MAP P.36

Albert Dock, L3. Bus: Salthouse Quay. http://beatlesstory.com. Hours vary, check website for details.

While shops selling Beatles products are ten a penny in Liverpool, most of them are not official, unlike this outlet associated with The Beatles Story museum. There's all manner of John, Paul, George and Ringo-themed miscellanea on offer here, from T-shirts and key rings to teddy bears in Yellow Submarine T-shirts – perfect for inspiring the next generation of devoted Beatle fans.

Liverpool Pictures

MAP P.36

Albert Dock, L3. Bus: Salthouse Quay. http://liverpoolpictures.co.uk. Daily 11am–5pm.

As the name suggests, this is the place to come to pick up beautifully drawn and painted pictures of Liverpool, produced by a number of local artists and spanning moody black-and-white photography, pop art prints of the *Cavern Club* in its Sixties heyday, a series depicting Antony Gormley's stunning *Another Place* installation on Crosby Beach, and much more besides.

Lost Soles

MAP P.36

Albert Dock, L3. Bus: Salthouse Quay. http://lostsoles.co.uk. Daily 11am–6pm, Sun until 5pm.

Having shot to regional fame on Instagram, local brand Lost Soles are a very modern success story. Originally specializing in rare trainers, they have since adjusted their focus towards menswear and kidswear, and are extremely popular on Merseyside for their graphic T-shirts, hoodies and sweatshirts – local footballers and musicians can often be seen wearing the latest styles.

Nature's Treasure

MAP P.36

Albert Dock, L3. Bus: Salthouse Quay. http://facebook.com/1naturestreasure. Daily 10am–6pm.

Handmade jewellery, homeware and artworks showcase the beauty of the natural world at this laidback emporium, with products carved from petrified wood, black shungite jewellery, gorgeous amethyst crystals and enough incense to fumigate the Liver Building. There are also ancient ammonite fossils, Indian religious statues and lovely bowls carved from rose quartz.

The Nest

MAP P.36

Albert Dock, L3. Bus: Salthouse Quay. http://thenestuk.co.uk. Daily 11am–5pm.

This showcase for local artists sells a wide variety of artworks and handicrafts, from prints of beautiful urban photography to handmade greetings cards and intricate drawings of British birdlife. You'll also find pots from local ceramic studio Baltic Clay, and fragrant soy candles from award-winning Birkenhead craftsman Owen Drew available to purchase.

Roly's Fudge

MAP P.36

Albert Dock, L3. Bus: Salthouse Quay. http://rolysfudge.co.uk. Daily 10am–5pm.

Beloved for more than 30 years for its sweet, crumbly, Devon-style fudge, Roly's Fudge apparently perfected its recipe in a copper cauldron in the kitchen of a farmhouse cottage. Over the decades it's expanded its product range to include rum and raisin, lemon meringue and cherry bakewell flavours, with a sea-salt infused fudge for those with a slightly more savoury tooth. There are also good vegan fudges available.

With Love from Liverpool

MAP P.36

Albert Dock, L3. Bus: Salthouse Quay.
http://albertdock.com/shop. Daily
9.30am–7pm.

All manner of Merseyside
memorabilia occupies the shelves
at this souvenir shop, from old-
fashioned Donald McGill-style
postcards to official Liverpool
FC scarves. There's also plenty of
non-Liverpool related miscellany
in stock, from Star Wars action
figures to ecofriendly tote bags and
reusable coffee cups made from
sustainable bamboo.

Restaurants

Cargo

MAP P.36

19 Princes Parade, L3. Bus: Galton St.
http://cargoseafoodrestaurant.co.uk. Tues–
Sun noon–10pm.

Ocean-fresh seafood is the order
of the day at *Cargo*, a popular
restaurant with a stylish and subtly
nautical decor. The monkfish, king
prawns and seafood risotto are all

highly regarded, while non-fish
eaters will find plenty to enjoy too,
from mango chicken to Cypriot
lamb stew. ££–£££

Delifonseca

MAP P.36

Brunswick Dock, L3. Bus: Galton St. http://
delifonseca.co.uk. Mon–Thurs 8am–6pm,
Fri–Sat until 7pm, Sun 9.30am–5pm.

Bistro with a changing blackboard
menu of European and British
delights, including Welsh black
beef meatballs, and roast pork
belly served with *lentejas* stew.
If you want to take some of the
delicious ingredients away with
you, check out the adjacent
foodhall, which has extensive
charcuterie, cheese, antipasti
and salad selections – perfect for
rustling up a picnic. ££

Gusto

MAP P.36

Albert Dock, L3. Bus: Strand Street. http://
gustorestaurants.uk.com. Mon–Thurs &
Sun noon–11pm, Fri–Sat 10am–11.30pm.

Britain's finest chain of Italian
restaurants has a particularly

Panoramic 34

attractively sited outlet on Albert Dock, with a sleek, atmospherically lit interior and a menu of classic Italian dishes. The Sicilian lamb and aubergine *caponata* is superb, as are the risottos and sourdough pizzas; carnivores will also love the huge burgers and steaks. ££

Hawksmoor

MAP P.36

8 Brunswick St, L2. Train: James Street. http://thehawksmoor.com. Mon–Wed 5–10pm, Thurs–Sat noon–2.30pm, 5–10pm, Sun noon–8pm.

The long-awaited Liverpool outlet of Hawksmoor, widely regarded as one of the finest steak restaurants in the UK, finally opened in late 2022 in the grand surrounds of the Grade II-listed India Buildings. The decor is beautiful, upholding the property's Art Deco heritage, but the highlight is the food: scallops in white port and garlic, Old Spot belly ribs, and chateaubriands as tender and delicious as they are enormous. £££–££££

Matou

MAP P.36

Pier Head, L3. Bus: Georges Pier Head. http://matou.co.uk. Mon–Thurs & Sun noon–11pm, Fri–Sat until midnight.

On the second floor of the Mersey Ferries terminal, *Matou* boasts great views of the Mersey on one side and the Liver Building on the other. The menu is a wide-reaching pan-Asian affair: there's Malaysian chicken satay, Chinese *sui mai* dumplings, Thai fishcakes, and of course salt and pepper chicken, which has become something of a Liverpool institution thanks to the influence of the Chinese community. £

Nova Scotia

MAP P.36

Mann Island, L3. Bus: Georges Pier Head. www.novascotialiverpool.co.uk. Mon–Thurs 9am–4pm, Fri & Sat until 7pm, Sun 9am–6pm.

On the northern edge of Canning Dock, this laidback spot is open throughout the day, drawing in tourists, freelance workers, students and everyone else with its international menu of comfort-food classics. Early in the day there's eggs on toast, fried options and breakfast brioches, while scouse, fish and chips and mighty burgers are among the favourites you can try later in the day. £

Panoramic 34

MAP P.36

Brook St, L3. Bus: Gibraltar Row. http://panoramic34.com. Tues–Sat noon–9.30pm, Sun until 8pm.

Views over Liverpool don't get much better than at *Panoramic 34*, a fine dining restaurant which sits on the 34th floor of the West Tower – in fact, this is one of the highest restaurants not just in the city but in the whole country. Just as spectacular as the view is the food, which fashions seasonal British ingredients into beautifully presented dishes like Cheshire pork cheek with Bramley apple and black garlic. ££££

Bars and nightlife

Baltic Fleet

MAP P.36

33a Wapping, L1. Bus: Dublin St. http://balticfleet.co.uk. Mon–Thurs & Sun noon–11pm, Fri–Sat until 11.30pm.

Restored, no-nonsense, quiet pub with age-old shipping connections and an open fire, just south of the Albert Dock. Local ales feature prominently on the taps, while in the warmer months the outdoor seating area is a nice spot to while away an afternoon. There's food on offer too, including burgers and meat and veggie scouse.

Brasco Lounge

MAP P.36

27a Mann Island, L3. Bus: Gibraltar Row. http://thelounges.co.uk/brasco. Daily

9am–11pm.

'Lounge' is the right word – this homely bar-restaurant, with its leather armchairs, rustic wooden tables and convivial atmosphere, is very homely. Whether you're after a pot of tea or fortifying coffee mid-sightseeing, or a beer or glass of wine after a day's adventures, this is a lovely place to put your feet up for a while. The cocktails are great, too – try the very British rhubarb, bramble and gin.

Carpathia

MAP P.36

30 James St, L2. Metro: James St. http://30jamesstreetliverpool.co.uk. Mon–Thurs & Sun noon–11pm, Fri–Sat noon–midnight.

Perched atop the iconic *30 James Street* hotel, *Carpathia* is an elegant rooftop champagne bar boasting some of the finest views over the docks and Liverpool's skyline. All the Three Graces are visible from up here, while the view to the restaurant inside, which elegantly wears its heritage as the former

headquarters of the White Line Shipping Company, isn't bad either. A stylish spot for a glass of champagne or a cocktail.

Invisible Wind Factory

MAP P.36

3 Regent Rd, L3. Bus: Dublin St. http://thekazimier.co.uk. Hours vary; check website for details of latest events.

From the creative minds behind local arts collective Kazimier (see page 68), this remarkable event space between Waterloo and Stanley Docks is one of the most exciting spaces in the city, serving as a music venue, workshop and art studio. The events programme is diverse, but electronic music dominates the nocturnal agenda; daytime events like yoga brunches are on hand to help you recover after a night's overindulgence.

Ma Boyle's

MAP P.36

7 Tower Gardens, L3. Bus: Cruise Terminal. http://maboyles.com. Mon–Fri 10am–11pm, Sat–Sun 9am–midnight.

Invisible Wind Factory

The Pumphouse

Sitting in the elegant Tower Building, this historic pub has played many roles since 1870, as a coffee shop and later an oyster bar. Today it's an atmospheric pub, which retains many period features like a stamped metal ceiling, wood-panelled bar and Victorian tiled floor. Live jazz every Saturday adds to the retro atmosphere.

The Pumphouse

MAP P.36

Albert Dock, L3. Bus: Strand St. http://greeneking-pubs.co.uk. Daily 11am–11pm. Recognizable from afar by its looming chimney stack, this redbrick building dates from 1874 and was once a pumping station for the Liverpool docks. Today it's a listed building and cosy pub, with a lovely wooden bar, John Lennon quotes plastered on the walls, and a decent menu of pub grub.

Smugglers Cove

MAP P.36

Albert Dock, L3. Bus: Salthouse Quay. http://thesmugglerscove.uk.com. Mon–Wed & Sun noon–midnight, Thurs until 1am, Fri–Sat until 2am.
Liverpool's nineteenth-century pirates were state-sanctioned privateers rather than smugglers, but it's fair to assume they had a taste for rum – and you will too, after you try the lychee daiquiri or spiced apple sling at this lively, atmospheric bar. Decked out in buccaneering style, with salty ropes, metal lanterns and dark wood everywhere, it's a fun place to kick off a city-centre night out.

Cafés

Bean

MAP P.36

Princes Dock, L3. Bus: Gibraltar Row. http://beancoffee.co.uk. Mon–Fri 7am–3.30pm.
Small local chain *Bean* are all about good coffee and local produce, and both are on offer at this coffee shop-meets-general store. A range of sandwiches and paninis are the perfect accompaniment to your brew; after you're done, pop into the shop to browse locally made confectionary, artisanal bread and cheese, and much more. £

Burnt Milk Hotel

MAP P.36

Albert Dock, L3. Bus: Salthouse Quay. www.burntmilkhotel.com. Tues–Sun 10am–11.30pm.
There's a roguish charm to this brick-walled café, self-declared as a magnet for "down and out reprobates, vagabonds, and rascals" – or at least, those with a penchant for natural wines and charcuterie plates. A sense of fun pervades, and it's easy to while away a couple of hours over a mezze board and a couple of glasses of wine, or a coffee and pastry. ££

Fab4 Café

MAP P.36

Pier Head, L3. Metro: James St. http://beatlesstory.com. Daily 10am–5pm.

A favourite refreshment point for those embarking or departing the Mersey ferry, this popular café is run by the team behind The Beatles Story museum (see page 35) and has photos of the eponymous Fab Four hanging on the walls. There's good coffee and tea, and a range of technicolour cakes in psychedelic hues which rival Peter Blake's famous razzle dazzle Mersey ferry. ££

Mrs Danvers Café

MAP P.36

Pier Head, L3. Bus: Georges Pier Head. http://facebook.com/MrsDanversCafe. Mon–Sat 10am–3pm.

Within the majestic Port of Liverpool building – one of the city's Three Graces – lies this tearoom, named for the imperious housekeeper in Daphne du Maurier's 1938 novel *Rebecca*. Though nowhere near as spectacular as the building's Baroque lobby, this is a pleasant and cosy space, with vintage armchairs and crockery evoking the 1930s. The afternoon teas are particularly good. ££

Peaberry Coffee House

MAP P.36

Albert Dock, L3. Bus: Salthouse Quay. http://peaberrycoffeehouse.co.uk. Mon–Thurs & Sun 9am–6pm, Fri–Sat until 7pm.

Taking its name from the coffee bean served here – a Brazilian 'peaberry' – you know that the minds behind this excellent coffee house are devoted to their ingredients. And so they should be, because they make for a delicious cup; there's also a rotating couple of guest coffees and a good range of tea, alongside delicious and extensive breakfast and brunch selections. £

Rubens

MAP P.36

Albert Dock, L3. Bus: Salthouse Quay. http://albertdock.com. Mon–Sat 8.30am–6pm, Sun 9am–6pm.

With several locations across Merseyside, *Rubens* is something of a local institution, and this newest addition to the stable has an unbeatable location in the Albert Dock. There's great Italian-style coffee, a range of classic British cakes like Victoria sponge and lemon drizzle, and a main menu of hearty comfort food – including the New York pastrami sandwich which gives the café its name. £

Tate Café

MAP P.36

Albert Dock, L3. Bus: Salthouse Quay. http://tate.org.uk. Daily 10am–5pm.

Having spent an hour or two traipsing around the world-class art galleries of the Tate Liverpool, you'll have earned the right to put your feet up. That doesn't mean an end to the art, though, thanks to this café which has been colourfully adorned by the British artist Peter Blake, in a similar style to his psychedelic *Snowdrop* Mersey ferry. There's a wide range of coffee and leaf tea, and the afternoon teas are superb. ££

Fab4 Café

Cavern Quarter and around

West of St George's Quarter and north of the retail quarter centred around Liverpool ONE, the Cavern Quarter is the name given to the web of streets around Mathew Street, home to the storied *Cavern Club* – the place perhaps more than any other associated with legendary rock band The Beatles. In truth, the tacky statues, endless loop of Beatles cover songs emanating from the bars, and swarms of camera-toting tourists mean it is impossible to imagine what this part of town would have looked like to a young John, Paul and co. Still, the reincarnated *Cavern Club*, along with the chance to visit still-standing ex-Beatle haunts like The Grapes (see page 57), make this a worthwhile stop for fans – who would come here even if it wasn't.

Cavern Club

MAP P.52

10 Mathew St, L2. Bus: Temple St. http://cavernclub.com. Sun–Thurs 10am–midnight, Fri–Sat until 2am. 10am–noon free; other times charge.

The self-styled "most famous club in the world" is the centrepiece of tourist hub Mathew St, and is where The Beatles established themselves as a live band in Britain after returning from their stint in Hamburg in 1961. Opened as a jazz club in 1957, the *Cavern Club* originally banned rock 'n' roll music – John Lennon's first group The Quarrymen were admonished for playing Elvis Presley's *'Don't Be Cruel'* at an early gig – but eventually became a fulcrum of the emergent Merseybeat scene. The venue has had a long and colourful history. Originally the cellar of a fruit warehouse, it had been used as an air raid shelter during World War II before opening as a music venue. Once its Sixties heyday had passed, the *Cavern Club* closed in 1973, and was filled in during work on a ventilation duct for the Merseyrail train network. Excavated again during the early 1980s, the club was eventually reopened on its original site in 1984, although several changes of ownership followed in the subsequent years. Today, the *Cavern Club* hosts live music every afternoon and evening of the week – a combination of Beatles tribute acts, singer-songwriters and indie rock bands. The stage area is almost as it was when The Beatles performed here, albeit rotated 90 degrees. The atmosphere is always high-spirited, and the quality of the musicians high, although it's extremely touristy and the glass-fronted wall exhibits – containing instruments, stage outfits and personal effects associated with The Beatles and other Liverpool musicians – can give the feeling that you're in a museum with a live band in the background, rather than a dedicated music venue.

Liverpool Beatles Museum

MAP P.52

23 Mathew St, L2. Bus: Temple St. http://liverpoolbeatlesmuseum.com. Daily 10am–6pm. Charge.

One Beatles museum was never going to be enough for Liverpool, and the waterfront's Beatles Story (see page 35) gained a new sibling in 2018 with the opening of the Liverpool Beatles Museum. The collection here, comprising more than 300 rare items, belongs to Roag Aspinall-Best, who, as the son of former Beatles road manager and assistant Neil Aspinall and half-brother of first Beatles drummer Pete Best, has a unique connection to the band. Items on display, spread over three floors, include George Harrison's Futurama guitar from the Hamburg years, Ringo's snare drum, and a pair of Lennon's glasses. Unusually, there is also space devoted to items associated with Pete Best and Stuart Sutcliffe, the band's original bassist, who sadly died in Hamburg in 1962 at the age of 21. As such, the museum will be of particular interest to those interested in the band's formation and early years – even if the addition of 'Pete' and 'Stuart' on the entrance doors alongside 'John', 'Paul', 'George' and 'Ringo' might raise a few eyebrows.

Cilla Black Statue

MAP P.52
Mathew St, L2. Bus: Temple St

Amid all the Beatlemania, it's easy to forget that Liverpool has produced many other music and entertainment stars. Among them is Cilla Black, who topped the charts repeatedly in the mid-Sixties and went on to become a popular television presenter. Unveiled in 2017 opposite the *Cavern Club* (where she used to work in the cloakroom before fame came calling) and the Magical Beatles Museum, this statue shows a young Cilla, grinning and arms aloft.

Eleanor Rigby Statue

MAP P.52
Stanley St, L2. Bus: Temple St.

This statue on Stanley Street depicts the fictional character of Eleanor Rigby from the 1966 Beatles song of the same name. The statue was created by the multitalented Tommy Steele, a contemporary of The Beatles who is considered to have

Performing at the Cavern Club

CAVERN QUARTER AND AROUND

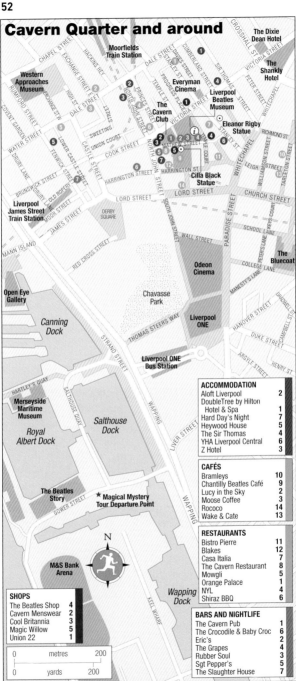

Cavern Quarter and around

ACCOMMODATION

Aloft Liverpool	2
DoubleTree by Hilton Hotel & Spa	1
Hard Day's Night	7
Heywood House	5
The Sir Thomas	4
YHA Liverpool Central	6
Z Hotel	3

CAFÉS

Bramleys	10
Chantilly Beatles Café	9
Lucy in the Sky	2
Moose Coffee	3
Rococo	14
Wake & Cate	13

RESTAURANTS

Bistro Pierre	11
Blakes	12
Casa Italia	7
The Cavern Restaurant	8
Mowgli	5
Orange Palace	1
NYL	4
Shiraz BBQ	6

SHOPS

The Beatles Shop	4
Cavern Menswear	2
Cool Britannia	3
Magic Willow	5
Union 22	1

BARS AND NIGHTLIFE

The Cavern Pub	1
The Crocodile & Baby Croc	6
Eric's	2
The Grapes	4
Rubber Soul	3
Sgt Pepper's	5
The Slaughter House	7

0	metres	200
0	yards	200

been the first British rock 'n' roll star; his '*Singing the Blues*' reached number one in 1957. The poignant sculpture depicts a woman in a coat and headscarf, sitting alone on a bench and looking towards a tiny sparrow which sits to her left. Her face, eerily, is blank – a reference, perhaps, to the song's line about "wearing the face that she keeps in a jar by the door."

Western Approaches Museum

MAP P.52
1–3 Rumford St, L2. Bus: Old Hall St.
http://liverpoolwarmuseum.co.uk. Daily 10am–6pm. Charge.

Towards the waterfront to the west of the Cavern Quarter, the Western Approaches Museum reveals an underground labyrinth of rooms, formerly headquarters for the Battle of the Atlantic during World War II. Far from a cramped, poky bunker, this was once home to some 300 people – a miniature subterranean town where people would eat and sleep for days at a time. Everything has been restored to be exactly as it would have been when the complex was abandoned in 1945. The massive Operations Room vividly displays all the technology of a 1940s nerve centre – wooden pushers and model boats, chalkboards and ladders – while you can get a feel for what

Eleanor Rigby Statue

life in here would have been like by touching the vintage phones and typewriters, trying on military jackets and handling replica papers and documents. The RAF Plotting Room contains maps, radio and navigation equipment, complete with sound effects, while the Road to War Room contains exhibits on the background of the Western Approaches Headquarters, and why it moved to Liverpool from its original location in Plymouth after France fell to the Nazis in 1940.

The enigmatic Eleanor Rigby

The story of Eleanor Rigby, the title character of the 1966 song of the same name, is one of the great pieces of Beatles Liverpool lore. The song, written by Paul McCartney for the band's album *Revolver*, initially featured the protagonists 'Daisy Hawkins' and 'Father McCartney', later to be replaced by the famous Eleanor Rigby and Father McKenzie. In the 1980s, a grave bearing the name 'Eleanor Rigby' was spotted in the graveyard of St Peter's Church in Woolton, less than a mile from John Lennon's childhood home; another tombstone, bearing the name 'McKenzie', was found nearby. McCartney has always maintained that he invented the Eleanor Rigby character, but has acknowledged that he may have seen the gravestone in his youth, for it later to emerge from his subconscious.

Shops

The Beatles Shop

MAP P.52

31 Mathew St, L1. Bus: Temple Lane. http://facebook.com/OriginalBeatlesShop. Mon–Sat 9.30am–5.30pm, Sun 10.30am–4pm.
Beatles tourists flock to this basement gift shop during their Mathew Street tours – with busts of John, Paul, George and Ringo above the entranceway, it's not hard to find. Vintage posters, vinyls and CDs are the standard stock-in-trade, but there's all manner of other miscellany to be had, from fridge magnets and Beatle bobbleheads to T-shirts and Lennon-style sunglasses.

Cavern Menswear

MAP P.52

9 Mathew St, L1. Bus: North John St. http://cavernmenswear.com. Mon–Sat 10am–6pm, Sun 11am–5pm.
If money is a mere detail in your pursuit of sartorial perfection, check out the selection at this high-end urban boutique, which stocks menswear from brands like Dsquared, Moschino and Prada. The prices can be eye-watering – if you wince at the thought of spending £160 on a T-shirt, give this one a swerve.

Cool Britannia

MAP P.52

33–35 North John St, L2. Bus: James St. 0151 236 7788. Daily 9am–8pm.
If your zeal for British-themed gifts and souvenirs extends beyond the Beatle belly of the Cavern Quarter – and indeed beyond the boundaries of Liverpool – you may enjoy this shop. It stocks a very wide range of items including, strangely, scaled-down red London buses and beefeater bears as well as Anfield Road signs, and Chelsea scarves alongside Liverpool and Everton ones.

Magic Willow

MAP P.52

8 Mathew St, L2. Bus: Victoria St. http://facebook.com/magic.willow.shop. Mon–Sat

The Beatles Shop

9.30am–5.30pm.

'Witches welcome' decrees a sign in this pleasingly rambling shop, which sells all manner of bohemian and esoteric items from incense burners to 'magical' healing crystals. Resident chihuahua Kiki can be seen modelling the latest quartz necklaces and bracelets, and the general chilled-out atmosphere makes this a nice place to duck into, have a browse and escape the Beatle bustle.

Union 22

MAP P.52

23 Victoria St, L1. Bus: Temple St. http://union22.com. Mon–Sat 9.30am–6pm.

Occupying the former Tetley & Co. headquarters in the impressive 135-year-old Union House, Union 22 is an independent boutique specializing in high-end men's fashion, although there's also an expanding women's range. Some of the products on offer include luxury swimwear from Beach Club Apparel, cashmere jumpers and polos from Bertolo, and quality jeans from Jacob Cohën.

Restaurants

Bistro Pierre

MAP P.52

14 Button St, L2. Bus: Whitechapel. http://bistropierreliverpool.co.uk. Mon–Sat 11.45am–10pm, Sun until 9pm.

For superb French country cuisine in a cosy setting, look no further than *Bistro Pierre*. The menu is based around hearty rustic dishes, like beef bourguignon, garlic and herb marinated lamb rump, and roast chicken suprême, while the fancier offerings include red pepper and couscous caviar and Prosecco and whiskey cured salmon. ££

Blakes

MAP P.52

Central Buildings, North John St, L2. Metro: James St. http://harddaysnighthotel.

com. Mon–Thurs & Sun 5–9pm, Fri–Sat noon–9pm.

Like the rest of the *Hard Day's Night Hotel* (see page 115) in which it sits, *Blakes* is rather more tasteful in its Beatles tributes than some of the other bars and restaurants in this part of town. Arty black-and-white photos of the Fab Four hang on the walls of a beautiful high-ceilinged room, which the menu doesn't quite live up to – though it's perfectly pleasant. Options include slow-braised beef, haddock and chips, and other British classics. Mains ££–£££

Casa Italia

MAP P.52

36–40 Stanley St, L1. Bus: Temple St. http://thecasaitalia.com. Mon–Sat noon–10pm, Sun noon–8pm.

Opened in 1976, and still in the same family after more than four decades of service, *Casa Italia* is a Liverpool institution. With its checked tablecloths, wrought-iron ceiling lanterns and tiled walls, it has the homely feel of an Italian trattoria, and the menu follows suit – it's mainly hearty pizzas and comforting pasta dishes, with an emphasis on traditional recipes and fresh ingredients. £–££

The Cavern Restaurant

MAP P.52

7 Mathew St, L2. Bus: Temple St. www.thecavernrestaurant.com. Daily noon–10.30pm.

Inside the *Cavern Club*, this is the place to come to refuel before or after catching a show at Liverpool's most iconic music venue – and like the club itself, the menu is all things iconic and British. Expect beautifully turned dishes like goat's cheese and pear, scouse stew, and rump of lamb with potato dauphinoise. ££

Mowgli

MAP P.52

69 Bold St, L1. Bus: Bold Place. http://mowglistreetfood.com. Mon–Thurs & Sun noon–9.30pm, Fri–Sat until 10.30pm.

Aloft and NYL

Bearing the unusual slogan 'Indian street food' – to which the menu here bears little relation – the food at *Mowgli* is nonetheless superb. The famous yoghurt-filled *chaat* bombs are the signature starter, the curries are rich and delicious, and there are some delicious spice-infused drinks; try the cardamom Old Fashioned. Food is served on a 'small plates', tapas-style basis. ££

Orange Palace

MAP P.52

9 Stanley St, L1. Metro: Moorfields. 0151 215 0051. Mon–Thurs & Sun 10am–8.30pm, Fri–Sat 9.30am–9pm.

Restaurant quality at kebab shop prices is a fair summation of this perennially popular place, cheerfully decorated with cartoon murals of Liverpool on the wall. The wide-ranging menu encompasses full English breakfasts, pizzas and even quesadillas, but the best options are the rice and kebab dishes. The two-course meal deal is good value, too. £

NYL

MAP P.52

1 North John St, L2. Bus: North John St. http://nyliverpool.com. Mon, Tues & Sun 6.30am–11pm, Wed & Thurs 5–11pm, Fri–Sat noon–1am.

In the elegant setting of the restored Royal Insurance Building (also home to the *Aloft* hotel; see page 115), this classy restaurant brings the flavours of the Big Apple to Merseyside with a menu that includes New York-style pizzas, vast steaks and burgers, and chicken wings, alongside European offerings. ££

Shiraz BBQ

MAP P.52

19 North John St, L2. Metro: Moorfields. http://shirazpalace.co.uk. Mon–Thurs & Sun 9am–11pm, Fri–Sat until midnight.

Charcoal-grilled meat kebabs are the speciality at this Mediterranean/Middle Eastern restaurant, though there's a good range of veggie options too – try the *hellim* kebab, made with Cypriot cheese, green peppers, mushrooms and onions. Be sure to leave some room for the hot fudge cake. £–££

Bars and nightlife

The Cavern Pub

MAP P.52

5 Mathew St, L2. Bus: Temple St. http://cavernclub.org. Daily 11am–midnight.

Under the same ownership as the *Cavern Club*, this pub and music venue is essentially more of the same without the historical interest. Good quality musicians play covers of classics from the 1950s onwards, and memorabilia is displayed in glass cases along the walls. The Wall of Fame outside may be of interest to music fans: each brick bears the name of a famous band or artist to have played at the *Cavern Club*, including the Rolling Stones, Arctic Monkeys, and of course the Fab Four themselves.

The Crocodile & Baby Croc

MAP P.52

19 Harrington St, L2. Metro: James St. 0151 255 1731. Daily 11am–midnight.

With live football, karaoke nights and live music, this traditional pub is always lively and offers a less touristy alternative to the Beatle bars of the Cavern Quarter. The two halves of the pub – the main 'Crocodile' bar and the smaller 'Baby Croc' room – are separated by a pleasant outdoor area.

Eric's

MAP P.52

9 Mathew St, L2. Bus: Temple St. http://facebook.com/ericsliverpool. Mon–Thurs 9pm–2am, Fri 7pm–3am, Sat 2pm–3am, Sun 9pm–2am.

Several Mathew Street venues have gone by the name *Eric's* over the years. The first played a crucial role in the Sixties Merseybeat scene, and the present-day incarnation, on the site of the original, has returned to its live music roots, with shows every night and free entry.

The Grapes

MAP P.52

25 Mathew St, L2. Bus: Temple St. http://blindtigerinns.co.uk/pubs/the-grapes. Mon–Fri noon–2am, Sat–Sun until 3am.

This pub, always overflowing with tourists, was a favourite haunt of The Beatles in their *Cavern Club* days. Certain elements of it, like the tiled fireplaces and checkerboard floor, haven't changed much. Certain others – like a huge wall sign pointing down to a sofa which declares 'The Beatles sat here' – definitely have, but that will only encourage snap-happy fans.

Rubber Soul

MAP P.52

9 Mathew St, L2. Bus: Temple St. http://facebook.com/RubberSoulMathewSt. Mon–Sat 10am–3am, Sun 10am–midnight.

This is the place on Mathew Street to keep the party going after things wrap up at the *Cavern Pub* at the weekend. There's live music every night and live comedy at weekends, which then give way to a rowdy dancefloor alive with the sound of rock, soul and disco.

The Cavern Pub

Sgt Pepper's

MAP P.52

4–6 Mathew St, L2. Bus: Temple St. http://
sgt-peppers.co.uk. Sun–Thurs noon–1am,
Fri noon–2am, Sat 11am–4am.

There are no prizes for guessing
the theme of this venue across
the road from the *Cavern Pub*,
but while Beatles covers are not
uncommon here, they are less
the main event than at its more
famous neighbour, and in some
ways this feels like more of a
proper music venue. With over
70 hours of live music per week,
it's a great place to catch a show
while you're waiting for dinner or
for the headline act at the *Cavern
Pub*.

The Slaughter House

MAP P.52

13–15 Fenwick St, L2. Metro: James St.
http://slaughterhouseliverpool.co.uk.
Mon–Thurs & Sun 9am–midnight, Fri–Sat
until 2am.

For some comic relief from the
overwhelming tourist crowds

The Grapes

of Mathew Street, head to this
legendary pub, which is the oldest
in Liverpool. The sawdust on
the floor is long gone, but it's as
popular as ever; big screens and
ample seating make this a great
place to watch live sport, while the
Laughterhouse comedy club (get
it?) downstairs is one of the finest
places in the city to catch local and
touring comedians.

Cafés

Bramleys

MAP P.52

29 Tarleton St, L1. Bus: Whitechapel. www.
bramleys-liverpool.co.uk. Mon–Fri & Sun
10am–5pm, Sat 10am–6pm.

Unfussy food, done well and
served with a smile, is what it's
all about at this unpretentious
café-restaurant. The toasties, eggs
on toast and baked potatoes are
all comforting, delicious and
cheap, while the fried breakfasts
are the perfect way to start a day's
touring the sights of the Cavern
Quarter. £

Chantilly Beatles Café

MAP P.52

8 Mathew St, L2. Bus: Temple Lane. 0151
236 0184. Mon–Sat 9am–5pm.

Within the Cavern Walks
shopping centre, this popular
café has guitars hanging from the
ceiling, an old-school jukebox
(one band are particularly well
represented), and wall space
liberally plastered with photos
and memorabilia relating to the
band – other local legends, like
comedian Ken Dodd, also get a
look-in. £

Lucy In the Sky

MAP P.52

Exchange St East, just off Dale St L2.
Bus: North John St. http://facebook.
com/lucyintheskyliverpool. Mon–Fri
8am–3.30pm, Sat 9am–2pm.

The pink neon signs and cheerful
decor make this café easy

Nightlife on Mathew Street

Instagram fodder, but it's not all about appearance. The food is simple but delicious, with the menu including good honest northern favourites like sausage barms (a type of soft white bread roll) and teacakes. £

Moose Coffee

MAP P.52
6 Dale St L2. Bus: North John St. http://moosecoffee.co. Daily 8am–5pm.
Beloved of locals for its enormous American and Canadian style breakfasts, this is the Dale Street branch of what is a small northern chain. The all-day breakfasts include 'Lone Star Moose' – a riot of steak, sausage and potato hash – and 'Coney Island', which combines a beef hot dog with pulled pork, melted cheddar and *pico de gallo*, a tomato and onion salsa. £

Rococo

MAP P.52
61 Lord St, L2. Bus: Lord St. http://

rococoffeeliverpool.com. Mon–Sat 9am–6pm, Sun 10am–6pm.
This indie café is housed in a historic building with a colourful history – it was once the head office of Radio Caroline, an infamous 'pirate radio' station, in the Sixties. Today it's a relaxed spot to grab a coffee and panini, a scone or custard tart, or a healthy salad. There's also beer and wine on offer. £

Wake & Cate

MAP P.52
13–17 Tarleton St, L1. Bus: Whitechapel. http://wakeandcate.co.uk. Daily 9am–8pm.
Run by a team of passionate patissiers with decades' experience in the industry, this bakery serves all manner of macaroons, gateaux and pastries, alongside savoury options like paninis and sandwiches. Everything is done with passion and care, an ethos which extends beyond the food to the selection of coffee, tea and smoothies. £

Ropewalks and around

Ropewalks is a rejuvenated former industrial district, whose warehouses and factories were once used to make rope for the many ships that docked in the waterfront. Today, the area retains much of its industrial aesthetic, but is now home to forward-thinking art galleries, creative spaces, vintage boutiques and cafés. Nowhere encapsulates this modern rebirth more than the beautifully proportioned Bluecoat Chambers on School Lane, which was built in 1717 as an Anglican boarding school for orphans and today houses a contemporary arts centre. Passing beneath the shadow of the modern Liverpool ONE shopping centre to Wolstenholme Square, you'll find *Penelope*, a huge modern sculpture of coloured plexiglass spheres on giant interwoven stalks, created by sculptor Jorge Pardo for the 2006 Biennial; it's especially striking when illuminated at night. Further to the east, past the shops and cafés of Bold Street, is one of the city's most striking buildings: the roofless husk of St Luke's Bombed Out Church. In the southern reaches of the Ropewalks, Liverpool's Chinatown is the oldest in Europe, while the extremely trendy Baltic Triangle is home to some of the city's coolest bars and restaurants, many housed in converted warehouses.

The Bluecoat

Liverpool ONE

MAP P.62

5 Wall St, L1. Metro: James St, Liverpool Central. http://liverpool-one.com. Mon–Fri 10am–8pm, Sat 10am–7pm, Sun 11am–5pm.

Contrasting with the independent cafés and boutiques of Bold Street to the east, Liverpool ONE, opened in 2008, is the heart of the city's big-chain retail scene. Covering some 42 acres, this vast, multi-venue cathedral to consumerism has changed the face of the city centre – and provided a significant boost to the local economy, with Liverpool now ranking among the UK's most popular retail destinations. The development includes two hotels – a *Hilton* and a *Novotel* – and some 170 shops and restaurants. The westernmost of six 'districts' is Chavasse Park, a green open space overlooked by a vast Odeon cinema; to the east, Peter's Lane and Manesty's Lane are home to high-end fashion retailers like Hugo Boss and Ralph Lauren, while once-derelict Hanover Street is home to some fantastic restaurants, including the flagship branch of *Lunya* (see page 66).

The Bluecoat

MAP P.62

8 School Lane, L1. Metro: Liverpool Central. http://thebluecoat.org.uk. Tues–Sun 11am–5pm.

One of Liverpool's most iconic historic buildings, the Bluecoat stands in stark contrast to the modern architecture of Liverpool ONE. Completed in 1717, this is in fact the oldest surviving building in central Liverpool, originally opened as the Bluecoat School, which moved to its present site in Wavertree in 1906. Today, the original Bluecoat Chambers house The Bluecoat, a cultural hub which claims to be the oldest centre for contemporary arts in the UK. Its galleries host a rotating lineup of British and international artists; past exhibitions include etchings by Tony Phillips, CONSCIOUS, an interdisciplinary piece by Suki Chan exploring dementia, and breathe, spirit and life, which addressed the Bluecoat's historical connection with the Transatlantic slave trade through themes of decay and rebirth.

Bold Street

MAP P.62

At the heart of the rejuvenated Ropewalks district is Bold Street, the city's finest shopping street, home to a great spread of independent and small-chain cafés, bookshops, vintage stores and more. Bold Street was one of the ropemaking streets which gave this neighbourhood its name – a 'ropewalk' is a long lane, along which individual strands of material were laid straight before being twisted into the huge ropes required by the sailing ships moored at the docks. It later became a residential street, with grand houses springing up in the Georgian era to accommodate those who had grown rich from trading in the docks. The street is named for Jonas Bold, who made a vast fortune not only in the sugar and financial industries, but also the slave trade. Perhaps the most significant feature on Bold Street is The Lyceum, a Neoclassical building dating from 1802 which started life as the headquarters of the first subscription library in England. In the centuries since it has assumed several roles, including a newsroom, gentlemen's club, post office, and, most recently, a bank. Repeated attempts by developers to bulldoze the Grade II-listed building proved unsuccessful despite it standing vacant for years; it is now a Chinese restaurant.

FACT

MAP P.62

88 Wood St, L1. Metro: Liverpool Central. http://fact.co.uk. Mon–Thurs & Sun 11am–9pm, Fri–Sat 11am–11pm.

'Film, Art and Creative Technology' is the name of the game at FACT, Liverpool's premier institution for cutting-edge creative culture.

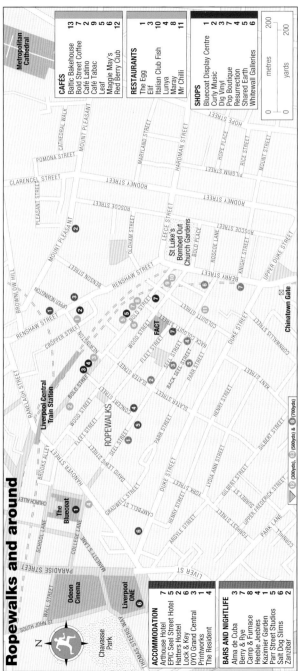

Ropewalks and around

CAFÉS
Baltic Bakehouse	13
Bold Street Coffee	7
Café Latino	2
Café Tabac	9
Leaf	5
Maggie May's	6
Red Berry Club	12

RESTAURANTS
The Egg	1
Elif	3
Italian Club Fish	10
Lunya	4
Maray	8
Mr Chilli	11

SHOPS
Bluecoat Display Centre	1
Curly Music	2
Dig Vinyl	3
Pop Boutique	7
Resurrection	4
Shared Earth	5
Whitewall Galleries	6

ACCOMMODATION
Arthouse Hotel	7
EPIC Seel Street Hotel	5
Hatters Hostel	6
Lock & Key	2
OYO Grand Central	3
Printworks	1
The Resident	4

BARS AND NIGHTLIFE
Alma de Cuba	3
Berry & Rye	7
Camp & Furnace	8
Heebie Jeebies	4
Kazimier Garden	1
Parr Street Studios	5
Salt Dog Slims	6
Zanzibar	2

metres 200
yards 200

FACT is housed in a grey tiled monolith somewhat at odds with its neighbours, the Victorian factories and warehouses of the Ropewalks district. Within, though, it's anything but bland: at any given time there are several things going on at once, from exhibitions of new artwork by local and international artists, to multimedia immersive virtual reality experiences, from live podcast recordings and poetry readings to free workshops and art classes. The complex is also home to the Picturehouse Cinema (http://picturehouses.com), which shows mainstream releases but is also the best place in town to catch international indie and art films which won't be gracing the screens of your local Odeon anytime soon.

St Luke's spire from Bold Street

St Luke's Bombed Out Church Gardens

MAP P.62

Leece St, L1. Bus: Bold Place. http://slboc. com. Gardens daily 10am–dusk; interior Sat–Sun 11am–dusk.

Among the most atmospheric sights in Liverpool is this ruined church, which was completed in 1832 but lost its roof to the German bombs

of the Liverpool Blitz in 1941. Remarkably, the rest of the structure remained almost completely intact, and now stands as a poignant memorial of the devastation of war while remaining a beautiful piece of architecture. Today the church holds occasional film showings, theatre and dance events, and artistic installations; a recent exhibit, From Guernica to Hiroshima: The Story of the Liverpool Blitz, was a moving illustration of the impact of World

Scouse: distinctive dialect and delicious dish

"We speak with an accent exceedingly rare" – so sang The Spinners on their Sixties hit '*In My Liverpool Home*', and they weren't wrong. The Merseyside accent, known as 'Scouse', is one of the most distinctive elements of the region, bearing little similarity to neighbouring northwest English dialects. The pronunciation can take some getting used to for non-locals, but you'll quickly come to recognise some of the local vocabulary: 'la' meaning 'lad' or 'mate', 'photy' for 'photo' (and endless variations on this theme), and 'boss' meaning 'good'. 'Scouser' is a common designation nationwide for people from Liverpool. The word comes from a local dish, also called scouse (originally 'lobscouse'), a stew of beef or lamb, potatoes and carrots which was popular as a cheap, nourishing and hearty meal for sailors before or after an extended trip at sea. Scouse remains a popular dish in Liverpool and pops up on the menus of many local restaurants – well worth a try during your stay.

The Dragons of the Pool

One of Chinatown's lesser told stories concerns the families of Chinese seamen who served in the British merchant fleet during the two world wars. Thousands of these merchant sailors perished during the wars; some of those who survived settled in Liverpool, married English women and had families. In 1945, the British government began the process of repatriating merchant sailors who had settled in Britain (some 6,000, according to a Chinese university study) – including those who had fathered children and had no wish to leave. Across the country, hundreds of children grew up without their fathers, believing they had abandoned them – many of the sailors were arrested on the street and taken directly to waiting ships, denying them the chance to bid their families farewell. Some of these unfortunate sons and daughters have formed a community group known as the Dragons of the Pool, aimed at raising awareness of their story and that of their fathers. In 2006, a plaque was unveiled at Pier Head which pays tribute to the Chinese merchant sailors for their service during the wars and reads, in Chinese and English, "For the children who never knew their fathers ... We hope nothing like it will ever happen again."

War Two bombing campaigns on ordinary civilians. Pop-up markets and yoga classes are regulars here.

Chinatown

MAP P.62

Beginning at the southeastern tip of the Ropewalks area, Liverpool's Chinatown is the oldest in Europe. The earliest Chinese visitors to Liverpool are thought to have arrived on a ship carrying silk in the 1830s, but they arrived in more significant numbers from the 1850s, after Alfred Holt's shipping line began employing Chinese sailors in an attempt to strengthen trade links with Chinese ports and overcome what had been a significant language barrier. Eventually, some of these sailors settled in Liverpool, establishing their own businesses to cater for the growing Chinese community, and Europe's first Chinatown. Its eastern entrance is marked by a vast *paifang* (monumental arch), which at 44ft tall is said to be the largest Chinese arch outside mainland China – though it's by no means the oldest, having been unveiled in

2000 during Chinese New Year. The arch was handmade by artisans from Liverpool's twin city, Shanghai, and features 200 carved dragons.

The rest of Chinatown is rather thin on tourist sights, being a mainly residential neighbourhood, but with its attractive shopfronts, jade green lampposts and bollards, and bilingual street signs, it has a pleasant atmosphere and a character distinct from the rest of the city. It is also, of course, the place to find Liverpool's best Chinese restaurants, among them *Mr Chilli* (see page 66).

Baltic Triangle

MAP P.62

Yet another former industrial area which has undergone a dramatic renovation, the Baltic Triangle is the city's most vibrant quarter, home to scores of creative industries, cool bars and cafés which have set up shop in the area's former warehouses and factory buildings. It may be low on tourist attractions, but is an atmospheric place to take a stroll and soak up the bohemian buzz; it also has some of the city's hippest eating and drinking options.

Shops

Bluecoat Display Centre

MAP P.62

50 College Ln, L1. Metro: Liverpool Central.
http://bluecoatdisplaycentre.com. Mon–Sat
10am–5.30pm, Sun noon–5pm.

This celebrated contemporary craft
and design gallery is worth a visit
just for a look around, as there are
some seriously impressive artworks,
handicrafts and homewares on
display. Many are also for sale and
make a fantastic gift or souvenir for
those on all budgets, whether you're
after a £400 brooch or a £10 candle
holder.

Curly Music

MAP P.52

38 Renshaw St, L1. Bus: Benson Street.
http://curlymusic.com. Mon–Sat
10am–5pm.

No visit to Liverpool would be
complete without a browse of a
music shop, and while the Cavern
Quarter has nothing to rival
the guitar paradise of London's
Denmark Street, it is home to the
city's finest music shop, Curly. This
is Liverpool's leading stockists of
Gibson guitars, played by both
John Lennon and George Harrison.

Dig Vinyl

MAP P.62

27–29 Bold St, L1. Metro: Liverpool
Central. http://digliverpool.co.uk. Mon–Sat
10am–6pm, Sun 11am–5pm.

Crate diggers could get lost for
days in the bottomless pit that is
Dig Vinyl, a legendary record shop
that has long been a stalwart of
Liverpool's music scene but moved
in 2019 to a new location on the
floor above *Resurrection*. From
rock and jazz to psytrance and
singer-songwriter, every genre you
can imagine is represented here; dig
around for long enough and you
may just find a rare gem.

Pop Boutique

MAP P.62

Shopping on Bold Street

110 Bold St, L1. Metro: Bold Place. http://
pop-boutique.com. Mon–Sat 10.30am–
6.30pm, Sun 11am–5pm.

What makes *Pop Boutique* stand
out among the bevy of vintage
stores on Bold Street is its range,
which includes not only refurbed
men's and women's attire but also
own brand and designer new pieces
as well as an ever-changing range of
vintage homeware.

Resurrection

MAP P.62

27–29 Bold St, L1. Metro: Liverpool Central.
http://resurrection-online.com. Mon–Sat
9.30am–6.30pm, Sun 11am–5pm.

The dramatically named
Resurrection is Bold Street's most
beloved vintage store, giving new
life to thousands of men's and
women's items which are packed
into a two-storey building. As well
as picking up some new threads,
you might even spot a celebrity;
local bands The Zutons and The
Coral are said to be regular patrons.

Shared Earth

MAP P.62

71 Bold St, L1. Metro: Bold Place. http://
sharedearth.co.uk. Mon–Sat 9am–6pm, Sun

11am–5pm.
Nowhere distils Bold Street's bohemian essence quite like this fair trade, ecofriendly and ethical-focused shop, which sells everything from carved wooden jewellery boxes to scented candles and bamboo socks. Everything is sourced from companies who treat workers well and only use sustainable products.

Whitewall Galleries

MAP P.62

49 Paradise St, L1. Metro: James St, Liverpool Central. www.whitewallgalleries.com. Mon–Sat 10am–6pm, Sun 11am–5pm.
Adding a dash of culture to the high-street chains and restaurants of Liverpool ONE, this art gallery exhibits and sells works by local, national and international artists, specialising in vibrant pop-art prints.

Restaurants

The Egg

MAP P.62

16–18 Newington, L1. Bus: Upper Newington. http://theggcafe.co.uk. Mon–Thurs 9am–9pm, Fri 9am–10pm, Sat 10am–10pm, Sun 10am–6pm.
Up on the third floor of a Victorian warehouse, this plant-strewn bohemian café serves excellent vegan and vegetarian food with good set-meal deals. Also a nice place for a chai. With seating around long wooden benches, it's a sociable kind of place, housed in one of the old Victorian warehouses for which the Ropewalks is renowned. £

Elif

MAP P.62

33 Bold St, L1. Bus: Bold Place. 0151 709 1561. Daily 11am–11pm.
Delicious barbecued Turkish meat and veg dishes are the order of the day at this atmospheric restaurant, with authentic, aromatic offerings like stuffed vine leaves and red peppers, spicy *sucuk* sausage, and hearty *güveç* stews. There's a good value lunch deal offering two courses for a reduced price. £–££

Italian Club Fish

MAP P.62

128 Bold St, L1. Bus: Bold Place. http://theitalianclubfish.com. Mon–Sat noon–10pm, Sun noon–9pm.
Proper Italian seafood place with a menu that adapts to what's fresh – try the *Sauté Di Maurizio*. There are also a few token meat and vegetarian dishes, all decent value. Over the road is *Italian Club*, its slightly cooler, younger sister. ££

Lunya

MAP P.62

55 Hanover St, L1. Bus: Bold Place. http://lunya.co.uk. Mon & Tues 10am–9pm, Wed & Thurs 10am–9.30pm, Fri 10am–10pm, Sat 9am–10pm, Sun 10am–8.30pm.
Gorgeous Catalan and Spanish deli-restaurant in the heart of Liverpool ONE, with a vast tapas selection and menus running the gamut from suckling pig banquet to vegan plates. *Lunya* is now a small local chain, with an outlet on the Albert Dock, but this was the original. ££

Maray

MAP P.62

91 Bold St, L1. Bus: Bold Place. http://maray.co.uk. Mon–Thurs & Sun noon–10pm, Fri–Sat until 11pm.
The ever popular *Maray* serves up a cosmopolitan small-plate menu which touches on American (buttermilk fried chicken) and Scandinavian (mushroom on rye bread) flavours but is mostly rooted in the Med and Middle East, with superb falafel, *fattoush* salad, and lamb shawarma dishes. With its bare bricks, upcycled benches and hanging bulbs, the aesthetic is pure hipster, and it's a nice spot to hang around for a cocktail afterwards. £

Mr Chilli

MAP P.62

Ordering at Lunya

92 Seel St, L1. Bus: Seel St. http://
facebook.com/Mr.Chilli.Liverpool. Mon &
Tues noon–midnight, Wed–Sun noon–2am.
Mr Chilli is widely held to be
the best Sichuan restaurant in
Liverpool, with famous for its fiery
dishes and good-value hot pots.
Adventurous gastronomes can try
unusual dishes like jellyfish. The
service can be a little brisk, but
that adds to the enjoyably lively
atmosphere. ££

Bars and nightlife

Alma de Cuba
MAP P.62
St Peter's Church, Seel St, L1. Bus: Seel St.
http://alma-de-cuba.com. Fri 2pm–2am,
Sat 2pm–3am, Sun 11am–11pm.
It may have far more candles now
than when it was a church – and
even more in the mezzanine
restaurant – but the mirrored
altar is still the focus of this bar's
rich, dark Cuban-themed interior.
There's a weekly 'Sunday Service'
brunch accompanied by a live
gospel choir, while there's live blues
and soul and carnival-themed
nights in the evenings.

Berry & Rye
MAP P.62
48 Berry St, L1. Bus: Seel St. http://twitter.
com/berry_and_rye. Mon–Wed 7pm–2am,
Thurs 5pm–2am, Fri–Sat 5pm–3am, Sun
5pm–1am.
You'll have to hunt hard – or ask a
likely local – to find this unmarked
bar, but once you're in it's a delight.
An intimate, bare-brick gin and
whiskey joint with knowledgeable
bartenders, turn-of-the-twentieth-
century music – often live – and
well-crafted cocktails. 'Whiskey,
blues, jazz & gin' is the strapline –
and that pretty much sums it up.

Camp & Furnace
MAP P.62
67 Greenland St, L1. Bus: Greenland
St. http://campandfurnace.com. Daily
10am–late.
The legendary *Camp & Furnace*
encapsulates the bohemian
blooming of the Baltic Triangle.
Housed in one of the district's
atmospheric old warehouses,
this vast space retains much of
its period character, with huge
chimney stacks and original
brickwork. Today, it's part bar, part
music venue and part restaurant,

with the Sunday roasts heralded as among the best in Liverpool.

Heebie Jeebies

MAP P.62

80–82 Seel St, L1. Bus: Seel St. http://facebook.com/OfficialHeebieJeebies. Mon–Fri 5pm–late, Sat–Sun 1pm–late.

It may not carry the hipster cachet of some of the Baltic Triangle's more self-consciously cool venues, but every Scouser worth their salt will have some good memories of nights misspent in *Heebie Jeebies*. A favourite of students and locals, this huge brick-vaulted room plays host to mainly indie and soul, with some live bands. Outdoor courtyard too.

Kazimier Garden

MAP P.62

32 Seel St, L1. Bus: Seel St. http://thekazimier.co.uk/kazimiergarden. Mon–Thurs 4–11pm, Fri–Sun noon–11.30pm.

The legendary *Kazimier* club closed its doors in 2016 and the organization turned its gaze towards producing multimedia shows for other venues, but the spirit of the club lives on at the trendy *Kazimier Garden*. With a super-creative vibe and a magical garden space decorated with upcycled furniture, this is a lovely place to watch a weekend day melt away over drinks, delicious veggie food and music.

Parr Street Studios

MAP P.62

33–45 Parr St, L1. Bus: Seel St. http://facebook.com/studio2parrstreet. Hours vary; check website for details.

Dynamic working recording studios – the UK's biggest outside London – hosting a long list of big names and home to a darkly stylish bar, *The Attic*, and *Studio2*, now an atmospheric venue for live performances. Check the website for details of what's on when.

Salt Dog Slims

MAP P.62

79–83 Seel St, L1. Bus: Seel St. http://saltdogslims.com. Mon–Thurs 5pm–2am, Fri–Sun 3pm–2am.

American-style bar that's a lot of fun, with a young, friendly crowd wolfing delicious hot dogs washed down with plenty of beers, backed by a solidly indie soundtrack. Upstairs is the supposedly secret *81 Ltd*, which rocks a Prohibition-era speakeasy vibe, though perhaps a tad self-consciously.

Zanzibar

MAP P.62

43 Seel St, L1. Bus: Seel St. www.zanzibarclub.co.uk. Hours vary; check website for schedule.

One of the best places in Liverpool to catch an intimate rock show, with a varied roster including up-and-coming bands and more established acts alike – local legends Miles Kane and The Coral are among the luminaries to have graced the stage at 'the Zanzi', as it is known hereabouts.

Cafés

Baltic Bakehouse

MAP P.62

46 Bridgewater St, L1. Bus: Bridgewater St. www.balticbakehouse.co.uk. Mon–Fri 9am–3pm, Sat–Sun 10am–3pm.

On the junction with happening Jamaica Street, in the heart of the Baltic Triangle, is this perennially popular café-bakery, which offers a delectable range of pastries, pies and pizza slices – try the 'spicy sweet', with nduja and honey. The coffee is good too, and the sourdough has been described as the best bread in Liverpool. £

Bold Street Coffee

MAP P.62

89 Bold St, L1. Bus: Bold Place. http://boldstreetcoffee.co.uk. Mon–Sat 8am–6pm, Sun 9am–5pm.

On Bold Street and after a coffee? Look no further than *Bold Street Coffee*, a friendly and well-run establishment which serves a wide range of espresso-style brews alongside lovely toasties, healthy salads and less healthy fry ups. There are also more substantial offerings like braised feather blade of beef and butternut squash risotto. £-££

Café Latino

MAP P.62

28a Bold St, L1. Metro: Liverpool Central. 0790 190 0739. Mon–Fri 10am–7pm, Sat 9am–7pm.

Family-run for more than two decades, *Café Latino* is a convivial spot to while away an hour or two over a coffee and a slice of cake (the fudge cake comes particularly recommended). If you're after something more substantial, there are decent pizzas and pasta dishes on offer too. £

Café Tabac

MAP P.62

126 Bold St, L1. Bus: Bold Place. http:// cafetabac.co.uk. Mon, Tues & Sun 9am– midnight, Wed–Sat until 1am.

Opened in 1974, *Café Tabac* is like a little pocket of Montmartre right at the end of Bold Street – but with a menu rooted firmly on this side of the channel. It proudly claims to be the only place in Liverpool where you can get bacon on toast at 8pm; other options include hearty English breakfasts and American-style pancakes. Tea, coffee and booze are all served too. £

Leaf

MAP P.62

65–67 Bold St, L1. Bus: Bold Place. http:// thisisleaf.co.uk. Mon & Sun 9am–10pm, Tues–Thurs 9am–11pm, Fri–Sat 9am–late.

For a welcome break from the ubiquitous artisanal coffee which seems to come out of the taps in this part of town, *Leaf* offers a wide range of loose-leaf teas alongside classic brunch dishes like eggs Benedict and *shakshuka*. By night it becomes a trendy bar, with live music, quizzes and jam sessions. £

Maggie May's

MAP P.62

90 Bold St, L1. Bus: Bold Place. www. facebook.com/MaggieMaysCafeBarLtd. Mon–Wed & Sat 9.45am–6pm, Thurs & Fri until 7pm.

Standing proud amid the hipster coffee shop epidemic which has engulfed Liverpool, Britain, and the entire world, *Maggie May's* is a welcome throwback, with its gingham tablecloths, friendly, unpretentious service, and simple, well-done food. Jacket potatoes, burgers, lasagne and the like are the bedrock of the menu, with the signature dish being a delicious home-style scouse. £

Red Berry Club

MAP P.62

10–14 Jamaica St, L1. Bus: Hardy St. http:// theredberryclub.com. Mon–Fri 8am–4pm, Sat 9am–5pm, Sun 10am–3pm.

With a lovely wood-panelled interior garlanded with vines, *Red Berry Club* offers coffee connoisseurs a range of beans from as far afield as Rwanda alongside a variety of home-cooked specials, with everything veggie or vegan. The breakfast cakes and pastries are particularly good. £-££

Leaf

Georgian Quarter and around

Nowhere serves as a better illustration of the wealth that flowed through Liverpool in the 18th and 19th centuries (and the stark disparity between rich and poor) than the Georgian Quarter, which, in a metaphor for much of Britain, remained as lovely as it ever was while poverty and degradation ravaged the rest of the city in the 20th century. Liverpool's stately Hope Street is the heart of the Georgian Quarter. It's bookended by the city's two famous cathedrals: the vast Anglican Cathedral, and the space-looking (though actually older) Metropolitan Cathedral, which serves the city's Catholic community. This area is also home to one of the city's premier cultural institutions in Philharmonic Hall, and one of its most enduring mysteries: the Williamson Tunnels.

Liverpool Cathedral

MAP P.72
Hope St, L1. Bus: Pilgrim St. http://
liverpoolcathedral.org.uk. Cathedral daily
10am–6pm. Free; tower and audio tour
charge.

The Anglican Liverpool Cathedral looks much more ancient than the Metropolitan Cathedral (see page 74), but was actually completed eleven years later, in 1978, after 74 years in construction. The last of the great British neo-Gothic structures, Sir Giles Gilbert Scott's masterwork is vastly impressive in scale and claims a smattering of superlatives: Britain's largest and the world's fifth-largest cathedral, the world's tallest Gothic arches and the highest and heaviest bells. Contemporary visual art adds to the unique feel of the cathedral, including a pink neon sign by Tracey Emin: "I Felt You And I Knew You Loved Me". The bell tower is the world's largest overall, and one of the tallest, looming at an impressive 331ft. On a clear day, a trip up the tower (Mon–Fri 10am–5pm, Sat 9am–5pm, Sun noon–4pm; charge) is rewarded by views to the Welsh hills.

Princes Rd Synagogue

MAP P.72
Princes Rd, L8. Bus: Upper Stanhope
St. http://princesroad.org. Tours Mon–
Thurs 9.30am–3.30pm, Sun by special
arrangement. Charge.

The perfectly proportioned Princes Rd Synagogue is home to the Liverpool Old Hebrew Congregation and is the oldest synagogue in Liverpool. Built in the familiar red brick found in so many of Liverpool's buildings, it is set apart by its stunning Moorish Revival architecture, with its octagonal turrets, rose window and spectacular Byzantine-style Torah ark. It is regarded as the finest Moorish Revival building in the United Kingdom, and its design has served as a blueprint for other synagogues all around the world. Visitors are welcome, but it's essential to book a place on a guided tour (40min), online or over the phone. After the tour, you'll be free to browse the exhibition in the annex, which showcases artefacts including silver Seder plates, beautiful Talmudic scrolls and choral manuscripts.

Sheppard-Worlock Statue

MAP P.72

Hope St, L1. Bus: Sugnall St.

This modern sculpture, designed by Stephen Broadbent and unveiled in 2008, sits halfway down Hope Street, slap bang in between the Anglican and Metropolitan cathedrals. It commemorates the lives of David Sheppard and Derek Worlock – Liverpool's Anglican bishop and Roman Catholic archbishop, respectively – who became known for their close co-operation in a city often rent apart by sectarian divisions. Fittingly, it is a dual sculpture, consisting of two 15ft 'doors' of black bronze, which bear the likenesses of the two men and abstract images of their respective cathedrals. Sheppard (1929–2005) holds the unique distinction of being the only ordained minister to play Test cricket; an accomplished right-handed batsman, he played in 22 Test matches for England between 1950 and 1963, high-scoring with 119 against India at the Oval. Derek Worlock (1920–1996) was appointed Archbishop of Liverpool in 1976, and held a different kind of national profile; one of his national television appearances was on the first ever edition of the BBC political programme, *Question Time*. He was acclaimed for his work in the community following the Toxteth riots and the Heysel and Hillsborough stadium disasters in the 1980s.

Philharmonic Hall

MAP P.72

Hope St, L1. Bus: Sugnall St. http://liverpoolphil.com.

'The Phil', as it is known locally, is the home of the Royal Liverpool Philharmonic, one of the first concert societies in the world when it was formed in 1840. The current building is much younger – an Art Deco construction opened in 1939 – after the original hall was destroyed by fire. The orchestra remains the oldest in the country and the only one to have its own hall; they put on regular performances here, but that is only a small part of the wider calendar, which also includes rock and pop acts, film screenings, and more.

Liverpool Cathedral and Georgian houses

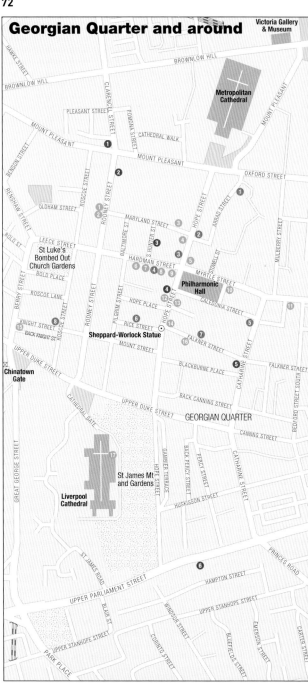

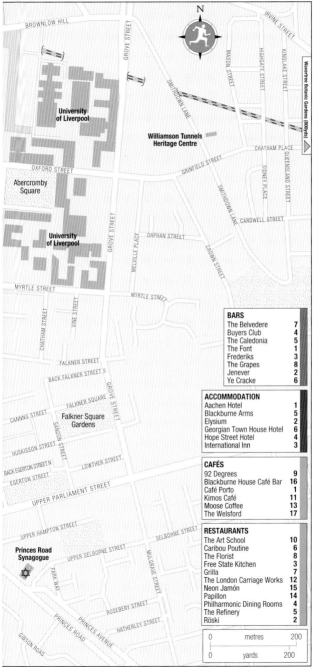

BARS

The Belvedere	7
Buyers Club	4
The Caledonia	5
The Font	1
Frederiks	3
The Grapes	8
Jenever	2
Ye Cracke	6

ACCOMMODATION

Aachen Hotel	1
Blackburne Arms	5
Elysium	2
Georgian Town House Hotel	6
Hope Street Hotel	4
International Inn	3

CAFÉS

92 Degrees	9
Blackburne House Café Bar	16
Café Porto	1
Kimos Café	11
Moose Coffee	13
The Welsford	17

RESTAURANTS

The Art School	10
Caribou Poutine	6
The Florist	8
Free State Kitchen	3
Grilla	7
The London Carriage Works	12
Neon Jamón	15
Papillon	14
Philharmonic Dining Rooms	4
The Refinery	5
Röski	2

0	metres	200
0	yards	200

The inside of the Metropolitan Cathedral

Metropolitan Cathedral

MAP P.72

On the hill behind Lime St, off Mount Pleasant, L3. Bus: Mount Pleasant. http://liverpoolmetrocathedral.org.uk. Cathedral daily 7.30am–6pm, crypt Mon–Sat 10am–4pm. Cathedral free; crypt charge.

After an original grandiose project of Sir Edwin Lutyens to outdo St Peter's in Rome was left incomplete (and eventually demolished in the 1980s), the idiosyncratically shaped Catholic Metropolitan Cathedral of Christ the King was built to Sir Frederick Gibberd's spectacular Modernist design. Consecrated in 1967, and pejoratively known as "Paddy's Wigwam" or the "Mersey Funnel", the building is anchored by sixteen concrete ribs supporting the landmark stained-glass lantern. The cherry on the cake is a ring of sharp pinnacles, which bring to mind Christ's crown of thorns. While the space-age exterior might not be for everyone, the inside is undeniably attractive, the stained-glass windows bathing the atrium in a spectrum of light. Ceremonial steps mark the approach from Mount Pleasant/Hope Street, with a café-bar at the bottom and four huge bells at the top.

All that remains of Lutyens' original design is the Lutyens Crypt (charge), accessible by a spiral staircase at the back of the main room next to the Chapel of the Blessed Sacrament. Set beneath redbrick vaulted arches, it's an atmospheric space with a beautifully symmetrical layout.

University of Liverpool

MAP P.72

Brownlow Hill, L69. Bus: Brownlow Hill. http://liverpool.ac.uk. Public access; individual buildings accessible by appointment.

Founded in 1881, the University of Liverpool is one of the United Kingdom's original 'redbrick' universities – the prestigious universities set up in industrial cities during their 19th century heyday (other redbrick institutions include Manchester, Bristol and Birmingham universities). Not for no reason is this part of town known as the 'Knowledge Quarter', and in a city of scientific world firsts, many of them took place in the laboratories of the university. It was here in 1894 that Sir Oliver Lodge made the first ever public radio transmission, and in 1896 made the first surgical demonstration of an X-ray. The architecture is suitably impressive for such a prestigious institution, with eye-catching modern steel and glass constructions complementing heritage pieces like the Victoria Building. The campus is open to the public, and anyone can wander around the public spaces and admire the architecture; to explore in greater depth, register for a self-guided visit on the website, where you'll also find campus maps.

Victoria Gallery & Museum

MAP P.72

Ashton St, L69. Bus: Brownlow Hill. http://vgm.liverpool.ac.uk. Tues–Sat 10am–5pm. Free.

The focal point of the University of Liverpool campus is the Victoria Building, a magnificent terracotta-hued structure said to be the original inspiration for the term 'redbrick university'. The building houses the Victoria Gallery & Museum, which often goes under the radar of tourists, but deserves more attention. The first floor contains a genuinely superb art collection, with a gallery dedicated to the beautiful wildlife paintings of John James Audubon and assorted pieces by world-renowned artists including J.M.W. Turner and Lucien Freud. The museum contains an exhibit on the heritage of the Victoria Building and university campus, alongside plenty to divert those of a scientific (and non-squeamish) bent. The 'Nightmares in a Bell Jar' collection comprises, well, nightmarish things in jars, from slithering reptiles to creatures of the deep, while 'Nasty Gnashers & Dreadful Dentures' takes a peek into the world of Victorian dentistry – which, to put it mildly, was no bed of roses.

Williamson Tunnels Heritage Centre

MAP P.72

Smithdown Ln, L7. Metro: Edge Hill, Bus: Smithdown Ln. http://williamsontunnels.co.uk. Fri–Sun 10.30am–4pm. Charge.

On the eastern edge of the Georgian Quarter lies one of Liverpool's great mysteries. During the first half of the 19th century, the wealthy tobacco merchant Joseph Williamson oversaw the creation of the Williamson Tunnels, a vast network of subterranean rooms serving a purpose which, to this day, remains a mystery. Williamson is an enigmatic figure; little is known about his early life, and there is speculation (albeit unproven) that the wild success of his tobacco industry may have been boosted, like many others of the time, by a sideline in slavery. By whatever means, Williamson became fabulously wealthy, and began to funnel some of his fortune into building projects along Mason St. For reasons unknown, Mason employed large numbers of labourers to tunnel extensively beneath and behind

Victoria Gallery & Museum

his housing projects, creating a network of vast excavations vaulted with brick and stone. The few contemporary references that exist to the tunnels do nothing to clear up the mystery; on the contrary, they depict Williamson himself as having been highly secretive about their purpose. Some people have suggested that their construction was born of a philanthropic desire to keep local people in a job – this theory is corroborated by bizarre reports that he would have men perform apparently pointless tasks, like moving piles of rubble from one place to another and then back again. Naturally, though, more colourful theories also abound, particularly the suggestion that Williamson belonged to an extreme religious sect that foretold the end of the world, and that the tunnels were to provide a refuge for this eventuality. Whatever the truth, a tour of the tunnels is a fascinating experience, if only as an illustration of the vast resources of one of Georgian Liverpool's wealthiest men.

Wavertree Botanic Gardens

MAP P.72
**Edge Ln, L7. Metro: Edge Hill. http://
liverpool.gov.uk/leisure-parks-and-events.
Daily 24hr. Free.**

To the east of the Williamson Tunnels, the Wavertree Botanic Gardens is a lovely spot for an afternoon stroll. This wide-open lawn, cut through with pathways flanked by cherry blossoms, was once home to the Liverpool Botanic Garden, which included a glasshouse home to exotic plants. This was sadly destroyed by a German bomb during the Blitz, with the surviving plants relocated to the botanical garden at Calderstones Park in Allerton. One historic building that does survive in Wavertree Botanic Gardens is the old curator's lodge, a Grade II-listed building which dates from the mid-1830s.

Cherry blossom trees at Wavertree Botanic Gardens

Restaurants

The Art School

MAP P.72

1 Sugnall St, L1. Bus: Sugnall St. http://theartschoolrestaurant.co.uk. Tues–Sat noon–2.15pm, 5–9.15pm.

Housed in the former Victorian Home for Destitute Children, dating from 1888, this superb restaurant combines heritage with a modern decor and a forward-thinking fine dining menu courtesy of head chef Paul Askew. Sample dishes include pheasant confit with quince jelly and Peterhead hake with Menai mussels. £££

Caribou Poutine

MAP P.72

8 Hardman St, L1. Bus: South Hunter St. http://cariboupoutine.co.uk. Tues–Weds 4–10.30pm, Thurs noon–10.30pm, Fri–Sat noon–11pm, Sun 2–9.30pm.

The UK is slowly but surely waking up to the charms of Canada's national dish, poutine, with a number of restaurants opening up in cities nationwide – and with fries and cheese curds, loaded with gravy and topped with any number of delicious combinations, what's not to like? This laid-back outlet is perfect for a quick meal – top your poutine with bacon, sausage, jalapeños, guacamole and more. £

The Florist

MAP P.72

24 Hardman St, L1. Bus: Sugnall St. http://theflorist.uk.com. Mon–Thurs & Sun 10am–11pm, Fri–Sat until midnight.

Vegans will love the plant-based menu at this attractive restaurant, prettily garlanded with an apt rainbow of colourful flowers. Dishes include Sri Lankan beetroot curry and pulled oat tacos; there's plenty for carnivores to choose from too, though, such as *massaman* beef ribs, sushi, and pork belly ramen. ££

The Art School

Free State Kitchen

MAP P.72

1 Maryland St, L1. Bus: Sugnall St. http://freestatekitchen.co.uk. Wed–Thurs noon–9pm, Fri–Sat noon–10pm, Sun noon–8pm.

Americana is the name of the game at this celebrated restaurant, which has the added bonus of a spacious lawn, perfect for alfresco dining in the summer months. Vast burgers, seafood chowder, Buffalo wings and New York-style salt beef sandwiches are among the menu highlights, while there's an extensive menu of gins, beers and cocktails to choose from, too. ££

Grilla

MAP P.72

22 Hardman St, L1. Bus: Sugnall St. http://grillarestaurant.co.uk. Tues–Sat 4–10pm, Sat 1–10pm, Sun 1–9pm.

As the name suggests, this Greek place is all about superb grilled meat and spit roasted dishes, from steak and eggs to lighter chicken wraps and salads. The *gyros* are particularly good, as are the mixed grills, served on a bed of fries. The portions are biblical, but they will happily box up any leftovers.

The London Carriage Works

The London Carriage Works

MAP P.72

40 Hope St, L1. Bus: Sugnall St. http://
thelondoncarriageworks.co.uk. Mon–Sat
11am–10pm & Sun 11am–9pm.

This superb British restaurant is the
jewel in the crown of the fantastic
Hope Street Hotel (see page 117).
Menu highlights include wood
pigeon with radish, parsnip and
damson, but it's worth coming
back for the lavish afternoon teas,
which are among the best you'll
find in Liverpool. £££

Neon Jamón

MAP P.72

Berry St, L1. Bus: Seel St. www.neonjamon.
com. Wed–Fri 4–midnight, Sat–Sun noon–
midnight.

The decor at this Spanish
restaurant, with its neon signs,
hammered copper and brick-and-
board walls, is rather hipsterish, but
the menu is traditional tapas done
beautifully. Try the *ibérico* pork
ribs, the chilli and garlic prawns,
and the semi-cured Manchego
cheese. ££

Papillon

MAP P.72

31 Hope St, L1. Bus: Sugnall St. https://
papillonhopestreet.com. Mon–Fri
10am–11pm, Sat–Sun 9am–11pm.

There's always a vibrant atmosphere
in this perennially popular
gastropub, which has a hipsterish
decor and a wide-reaching menu
of modern British bistro food done
well. Highlights include the pulled
chicken massaman curry with
coconut rice, while veggie options
include a delicious red pepper and
toasted hazelnut pesto tagliatelle.
Always popular, particularly for
weekend brunch, so booking ahead
is advisable. ££

Philharmonic Dining
Rooms

MAP P.72

36 Hope St, L1. Bus: Sugnall St. http://
nicholsonspubs.co.uk. Mon–Sat 11am–
midnight & Sun 11am–11pm.

Across the road from its namesake,
Philharmonic Hall, this pub dates
back to 1900. It is famous for
its grand Victorian interiors, in
particular the bathrooms, decked out

in colourful tiles and red marble. The food is good too: a classic British pub menu of full English breakfasts, fish and chips, steaks and burgers. There's even a separate pie menu. ££

The Refinery

MAP P.72

Josephine Butler Building, Hope St, L1. Bus: Sugnall St. http://therefinery-liverpool.co.uk. Daily 9am–11pm.

Housed in a rather ugly modern building that jars somewhat with its stately Georgian surroundings, *The Refinery* makes up for it with a stylish interior and a menu of well-done international dishes, from haddock and chips to lamb kofta skewers. ££–£££

Röski

MAP P.72

16 Rodney St, L1. Bus: Rodney St. http://roskirestaurant.com. Tues 6–9.30pm, Wed–Sat noon–2pm, 6–9.30pm.

'Modern British' is the menu mission statement at this acclaimed spot by Anton Piotrowski, whose previous accolades include a Michelin star. The set lunch is decent value and includes artfully presented dishes like guinea fowl with pearl barley and fermented pear sorbet. £££–££££

Bars

The Belvedere

MAP P.72

5 Sugnall St, L1. Bus: Falkner St. http://facebook.com/belvedereliverpool. Daily noon–11pm.

Teeny-tiny two-roomed backstreet pub, built in 1836 on the site of a former pleasure garden; to this day, punters spill outside when the sun shines. Changing ales and craft beers, including brews from Liverpool's microbreweries, and a splendid selection of gin.

Buyers Club

MAP P.72

24 Hardman St, L1. Bus: South Hunter St.

http://buyers-club.co.uk. Mon–Sat noon–midnight, Sun 1–11pm.

Achingly trendy wine and cocktail bar, with a particularly interesting wine list which tends towards natural and low-intervention wines, which are made with no or minimal chemical additions. There's a welcome beer garden, where regular music parties and BBQs are held in the warmer months.

The Caledonia

MAP P.72

22 Caledonia St, L1. Bus: Sugnall St. http://thecaledonialiverpool.com. Mon–Thurs & Sun noon–midnight, Fri–Sat noon–1am.

There's a great selection of craft beers and cask ales at this pub, which, with its upright piano and bookshelf corner, has a lovely homely feel; it's also so pup-friendly that it has its own branded dog biscuits. What's more, this is a vegan pub – a rare thing indeed – and there's a great selection of plant-based Californian cuisine. Regular live music nights.

The Font

MAP P.72

1 Arrad St, L7. Bus: Mount Pleasant. http://fontbar.co.uk. Mon–Sat 11am–11pm and Sun noon–10.30pm.

Popular with students, this hipsterish bar is great for cheap cocktails and boozy milkshakes, as well as slap-up fried breakfasts and burgers that are much better for the soul than the arteries.

Frederiks

MAP P.72

32 Hope St, L1. Bus: Arrad St. http://frederikshopestreet.com. Tues 4pm–1am, Weds 4pm–midnight, Thurs noon–1am, Fri noon–2am, Sat 11am–2am, Sun noon–midnight.

Halfway between Liverpool's two cathedrals lies this stylish church to the gods of alcohol and jazz. There's a pleasing mid-century modern decor, a fantastic selection of cocktails, gin and craft beer, and live jazz every Tuesday.

Ye Cracke

MAP P.72

13 Rice St, L1. Bus: South Hunter St. http://facebook.com/yecracke. Daily noon–11.30pm, Fri–Sat until 12.30am.
One of many Liverpool boozers that proudly claim to be a former haunt of The Beatles – in particular, this was a favourite hangout of John and Cynthia Lennon's. The history goes back much further, though, to the 19th century. The oldest part of the pub, the 'War Office', has a document on the wall explaining how locals would come here to discuss the Boer War between 1899–1902.

Cafés

92 Degrees

MAP P.72

24 Hardman St, L1. Bus: Arrad St. http://92degrees.coffee. Mon–Fri 7.45am–6pm, Sat 9am–7pm, Sun 10am–6pm.
True new-wave coffee connoisseurs flock to this café and roastery, which takes a modishly particular approach to making the perfect brew (no prizes for guessing where the name comes from). The good news is even the biggest coffee snobs will be impressed by the results. Regular live music, dance and poetry events too. £

Blackburne House Café Bar

MAP P.72

Blackburne Place, off Hope St, L8. Bus: Falkner St. http://blackburnehouse. co.uk. Mon & Fri 9am–4pm, Tues–Thurs 9am–8pm.
On the ground floor of the headquarters of Blackburne House, a local charity supporting vulnerable women, this café offers a great and reasonably priced selection of fresh salads, quiches, soups and sandwiches, and a nice selection of coffee and tea. £

Café Porto

MAP P.72

Mezzanine Café at the Liverpool Cathedral

The Grapes

MAP P.72

60 Roscoe St, L1. Bus: Falkner St. 0794 988 8700. Mon 4–11pm, Tues–Sun 11am–11pm.
Not to be confused with the pub of the same name near the Cavern Club (see page 50), this is much less touristy and much more a place to meet the locals. Real ale fans will enjoy the wide selection on offer, though as the historic 'noted wines and spirits' sign outside points out, that's only part of the story. There's also live jazz every Sunday.

Jenever

MAP P.72

29a Hope St, L1. Bus: South Hunter St. http://jeneverginbar.co.uk. Wed–Thurs 3–11pm, Fri–Sat 2pm–midnight, Sun 2–10.30pm.
Gin lovers rejoice: this voguish bar stocks no fewer than 120 varieties of 'Mother's Ruin' alongside the eponymous jenever, gin's Dutch predecessor. Pop in for a drink or two, or serious connoisseurs may want to book a tasting experience, which sees you tasting four varieties while you enjoy an informative history lesson.

14 Rodney St, L1. Bus: South Hunter St. http://cafeporto.co.uk. Tues–Fri noon–midnight, Saturday 3pm–midnight
A little slice of Portugal in the genteel surrounds of Rodney Street, this little café is a lovely spot for a glass or two of Portuguese wine or a coffee and a *pastel de nata*. There's food on offer too, including tapas-style light bites – try the *bolinhos de bacalhau* (salt cod fishcakes). ££

Kimos Café

MAP P.72

6 Myrtle St, L1. Bus: Sugnall St. http://kimos.co.uk. Mon–Fri 8am–11pm, Sat–Sun 10am–10pm.
There's fantastic value to be found at this cheerful café (note the steady stream of students), which serves a wide range of Mediterranean dishes from falafel and hummus mezes to *ful medames* (fava bean stew). The full English breakfast is also well regarded. £

Moose Coffee

MAP P.72

88 Federation House, Hope St, L1. Bus: South Hunter St. http://moosecoffee.co. Daily 9am–5pm.
This northwest chain has a couple of outlets in Liverpool (the other is at 6 Dale St), and specializes in big, North American-style breakfasts – the blueberry pancakes and French toast are particularly good. The food menu is huge – there are eight eggs Benedict options alone – but the coffee menu, all high quality, is refreshingly concise. £–££

The Welsford

MAP P.72

Anglican Cathedral, L1. Bus: James St. http://liverpoolcathedral.org.uk. Mon–Fri 11.45am–3pm, Sat 11.30am–4.30pm, Sunday noon–4pm.
Beneath the rib vaults of Liverpool's Anglican Cathedral, this informal café-restaurant is a great place to stop in for a coffee and a slice of cake after some sightseeing. Larger meals are also available, including a delicious scouse stew. For a different view over the cathedral, try the *Mezzanine Café* upstairs. £

Moose Coffee

Sefton Park and Lark Lane

No park in Liverpool occupies such a fond place in locals' hearts as Sefton Park, as pleasing a triumph of Victorian park landscaping as any outside London. Leafy Lark Lane is among the most pleasant corners of Liverpool, home to superb independent cafés, bars and restaurants, as well as some one-of-a-kind boutiques and arts hubs. This part of suburban south Liverpool will also be of interest to Beatles fans, as the area in which all four band members grew up; the childhood homes of John Lennon and Paul McCartney are now National Trust properties, atmospherically restored to appear as they would have done when the young musicians lived there. This is also where you'll find Strawberry Field and Penny Lane, which went on to inspire Lennon and McCartney respectively to write two of the most iconic Beatles songs.

Sefton Park

MAP P.84
Mossley Hill Dr, L17. Bus: York Avenue.
http://liverpool.gov.uk/leisure-parks-and-events. Daily 24hr. Free.

Bandstand in Sefton Park

Once a wooded deer park, the area around Sefton Park fell into disuse between the 17th and 19th centuries, until 1872 when the park was opened as part of a wider push to cultivate more green spaces for the benefit of the health of the wider population. A collaboration by local architect Lewis Hornblower and French landscape architect Édouard André, the park is 235 acres of gorgeous lakes, tree-shaded paths and daffodil fields – a gorgeous place to pass an hour or two of an afternoon. Looming over the northwest corner of the park is the Sefton Park Obelisk, built in red granite in honour of the 19th-century cotton broker, philanthropist and MP Samuel Smith. Close to the middle of the park is the Shaftesbury Memorial Fountain, also known as Eros – a replica of the fountain of the same name in London's Trafalgar Square, built in honour of Anthony Ashley Cooper, Earl of Shaftesbury, who was a famous philanthropist during the Victorian era. Continuing southeast in this direction, you will

Palm House

reach the Palm House and then, on the eastern edge of the park, the Fairy Glen – an enchanting corner of woodland grottoes, streams and gentle waterfalls.

Palm House

MAP P.84

In the centre of the park. http://palmhouse. org.uk. Daily 10am–4pm. Free.

The focal point of Sefton Park is the lovely Palm House, a stately Victorian greenhouse home to hundreds of weird and wonderful plants from five continents of the globe, including more than 20 varieties of palm and 32 orchids. Notable species include *Chamaerops humilis*, the only native European palm, and a 100-year-old date palm tree. Bird of paradise plants, angel's trumpets and bougainvillea provide a vibrant splash of colour to proceedings. The conservatory that stands today replaced a Band Pavilion in 1896; a gift from publishing magnate Henry Yates Thompson, it was designed by MacKenzie & Moncur, Ltd. The same company had built the famous Temperate House in Kew Gardens a couple of decades earlier; the Palm House, while nowhere near as large as its Kew counterpart, is arguably more attractive: an elegant three-tiered octagonal dome of glass and white-painted metal. Each of the octagon's eight edges has its own statue, each depicting either a famous explorer, botanist or navigator; examples include Charles Darwin, Christopher Columbus and Portugal's Prince Henry the Navigator.

Princes Park

MAP P.84

Princes Rd, L15. Bus: Belvidere Rd. http:// liverpool.gov.uk/leisure-parks-and-events. Daily 24hr. Free.

It may not be as large or as locally beloved as its neighbour Sefton Park to the east, but Princes Park is just as lovely a spot to while away an afternoon. Opened in 1842, the park was designed in part by Joseph Paxton, an MP, gardener and architect who would go on to be the brains behind London's Crystal Palace, built for the Great Exhibition of 1851. Paxton's other great contribution

Sefton Park and around

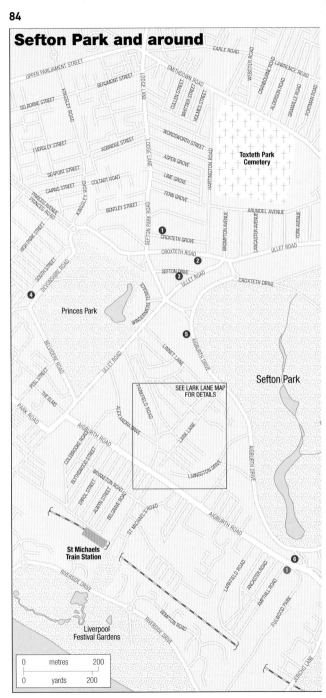

Toxteth Park Cemetery

Princes Park

Sefton Park

SEE LARK LANE MAP
FOR DETAILS

St Michaels
Train Station

Liverpool
Festival Gardens

| 0 | metres | 200 |
| 0 | yards | 200 |

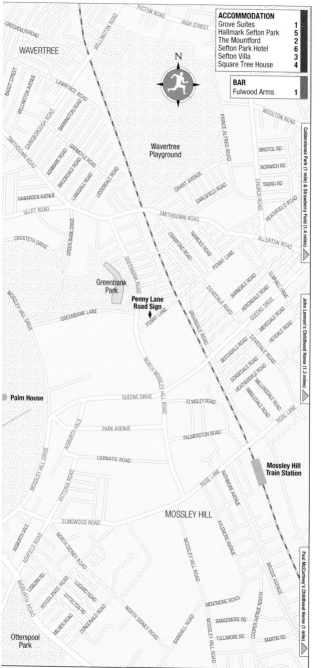

ACCOMMODATION
Grove Suites	1
Hallmark Sefton Park	5
The Mountford	2
Sefton Park Hotel	6
Sefton Villa	3
Square Tree House	4

BAR
Fulwood Arms	1

to history was his cultivation, while serving as a gardener at Derbyshire's Chatsworth House, of the Cavendish banana, now the most popular in the Western world. Circled by trees, bisected by walking trails, dotted with wooded patches and set around an off-centre serpentine lake, Princes Park would prove influential on the design of the later parks, including Sefton Park. The park has had a colourful history, home at various times to First World War rifle battalions, a Doric Lodge (destroyed during the Blitz) and the home of Unitarian philosopher James Martineau. In a patch of trees to the north of the lake is a touching gravestone to one Judy the Donkey (1905–1926), "who, during 21 years' service in this park, was the children's friend."

Lark Lane

MAP P.86
Lark Lane, L17. Bus: Lark Lane.

After a day enjoying the fresh air in Sefton Park or Princes Park, Lark Lane is just the place to retire for a long lunch, dinner, or some evening drinks – or, indeed, all three. This laidback neighbourhood is home to some of Liverpool's finest independent food and drink outlets where it's easy to watch the hours melt away. The hub of the street, and the starting point for many a legendary night out, is *The Albert*, a traditional pub in a former Victorian villa which was fully spruced up (while retaining its retro decor) in 2017. A short way south of *The Albert*, on the opposite side of the road, is perhaps Lark Lane's most beloved restaurant, *Maranto's* – a family-run Italian American outlet in a Grade II-listed building, which claims to have brought BBQ ribs to Liverpool back in 1985.

Lark Lane is not all about eating and making merry. The area has long had a reputation as a centre

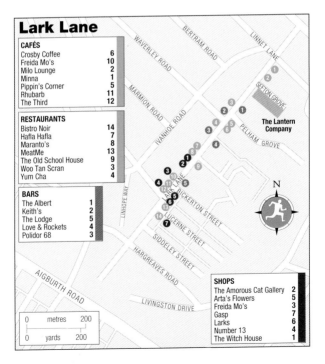

Lark Lane

CAFÉS
Crosby Coffee	6
Freida Mo's	10
Milo Lounge	2
Minna	1
Pippin's Corner	5
Rhubarb	11
The Third	12

RESTAURANTS
Bistro Noir	14
Hafla Hafla	7
Maranto's	8
MeatMe	13
The Old School House	9
Woo Tan Scran	3
Yum Cha	4

BARS
The Albert	1
Keith's	2
The Lodge	5
Love & Rockets	4
Polidor 68	3

SHOPS
The Amorous Cat Gallery	2
Arta's Flowers	5
Freida Mo's	3
Gasp	7
Larks	6
Number 13	4
The Witch House	1

The Lantern Company

N

0	metres	200
0	yards	200

Toxteth Park Cemetery

for bohemian lifestyles, and the arts are alive and well here. Arts Hub 47 (http://artshub47.co.uk; Wed–Sat 11am–5pm, Sun 11am–3pm), just off the south of Lark Lane on Aigburth Road, exhibits and sells work by local artists across a variety of different mediums, from crochet to ceramics. The Lantern Company (http://lanterncompany.co.uk; check website for latest events), who have their office at the northern end of Lark Lane in the Old Police Station, not only produce incredible lantern art but also hold regular art classes, from stained glass workshops to pottery sessions.

Toxteth Park Cemetery
MAP P.84
Smithdown Rd, L15. Bus: Granville Rd. http://toxtethparkcemetery.co.uk. Daily 24hr. Free.
To the north of Sefton Park, Toxteth Park Cemetery has become the final resting place of many prominent Liverpudlians since it opened in 1856. Famous gravestones here include that of Mary Billinge (d. 1863), who lived to the ripe old age of 112 years and six months and was

known, probably for good reason, as Liverpool's oldest woman; and 'Honest' John McKenna, an Irishman who was the first manager of Liverpool Football Club between 1892 and 1896. A derelict Anglican church is a somewhat affecting, if rather forlorn, feature of an otherwise pleasant spot for a stroll.

The northern end of Penny Lane

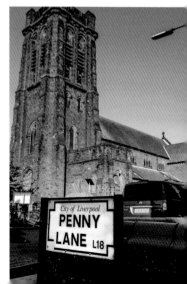

The replica gates at Strawberry Field

Penny Lane

Surely the most famous single road in Liverpool, if not the United Kingdom, Penny Lane was immortalized by The Beatles song of the same name in 1967. Written primarily by Paul McCartney, the song actually conflates several scenes, not all from Penny Lane itself, which McCartney remembered from his childhood bus journeys to Lennon's house and into Liverpool – he would change buses at Penny Lane interchange, where "the pretty nurse is selling poppies from a tray". The famous barbershop from the first verse is still there (it's called Tony Slavin), although the "fireman with an hourglass" appears to have relocated in the half-century since the song was written. The Magical Mystery Tour (see page 35) takes in Penny Lane, but for the sake of safety (and the sanity of local drivers and residents), does not stop near the interchange, but rather at the quieter southern end of the road – it's here that you'll find the most elaborately doodled-on Penny Lane road signs (Paul McCartney himself is said to have scribbled his name on one of them).

Calderstones Park

Calderstones Rd, L18. Bus: Calderstones Rd. http://liverpool.gov.uk/leisure-parks-and-events. Daily 24hr. Free.

Stonehenge may take the crown of Britain's most famous megalithic monument, but many people are unaware that a park in south Liverpool is home to something said to be even older. Calderstones Park, just to the west of Strawberry Field, takes its name from the Calder Stones: six Neolithic boulders thought to have once made up a dolmen, a kind of megalithic tomb. Unfortunately, the years have not been kind to the stones, which have variously endured graffiti, being ground up for cement, and, until recently, being kept away from the weather in a stuffy greenhouse which, far from preserving them, contributed to their deterioration. Happily, the stones are now on display under a new pavilion, protected from the rain but allowed to breathe. Other highlights of Calderstones Park include a pleasant lake, home to geese, ducks and fish, and the Georgian Calderstones Mansion House, which includes a café, ice cream parlour and children's story area.

Strawberry Field

Beaconsfield Rd, L25. Bus: Beaconsfield Rd. http://strawberryfieldliverpool.com. Daily Apr–Oct 9am–7pm, Nov–Mar 9am–5pm; last entry to exhibition 1hr before closing. Charge.

Once a grand Gothic mansion home to George Warren, a wealthy businessman who had made his fortune in shipping, Strawberry Field was sold in 1934 to the Salvation Army, who operated it as a children's home. A young John Lennon, who grew up down the road at 251 Menlove Avenue, would look forward to the garden party that was held here each summer; it was later said that he also used to scale the garden walls to play with the children. Whatever the true extent of Lennon's experiences here, the place clearly left an impression, as he saw fit to pay homage to it in 1967's 'Strawberry Fields Forever' – a double A-side with McCartney's 'Penny Lane', another song named for a location not far from here. The original house was demolished in 1973 and replaced by a custom-built children's home, which continued operating until 2005. The Salvation Army continued to use the centre as a church, but the site had never been open to the public until September 2019, when it reopened as a training centre for young people with learning disabilities, as well as a rather expensive café and a visitor centre with a small exhibition telling the story of the history of the site, John Lennon's connection with it, and the writing and recording of the famous song. There's an informative audio tour to complement the videos projected on the wall, which consist mainly of archival interview footage with the likes of Lennon,

McCartney and George Martin. For most visitors, though, the star attraction is out in the garden: the original Strawberry Field gate, stolen in 2000 but discovered after the thief tried to sell it to an eagle-eyed scrap metal dealer. This is the real gate – the one visible from the road is a replica. The Strawberry Field experience is a little expensive (especially if you add in the ticket for the psychedelic bus from Albert Dock), but that won't put off Beatle fans who finally have the chance to walk on hallowed turf.

John Lennon's Childhood Home

251 Menlove Avenue, L25. Bus: Vale Rd. http://nationaltrust.org.uk/beatles-childhood-homes. Daily June–Sept, Oct–May Wed–Sun; tours only, times vary. Charge.

Though this was not John Lennon's first home in Liverpool, it was here – where he lived with his Aunt Mimi and Uncle George – that became the house most associated with him in Liverpool. John had originally lived with his mother Julia, from whom he learned to play the banjo, but her

Mendips

20 Forthlin Road

personal problems – John would later say she "couldn't deal with life" – led to social services handing him over to her sister Mimi. Known as 'Mendips', this grey semi-detached house is bigger and more upmarket than the McCartney family home. Both are owned by the National Trust and are now museums which have been renovated to look as they would have when John and Paul lived in them. If they are notable for anything, it is their ordinariness – by themselves they are vaguely interesting time capsules of mid-century, lower middle class British life, but in their context they are testament to the way in which genius can emerge from an unlikely milieu of brown armchairs, flock wallpaper and lampshades with fringes.

Paul McCartney's Childhood Home

20 Forthlin Rd, L18. Bus: Forthlin Rd. http://nationaltrust.org.uk/beatles-childhood-homes. Daily June–Sept, Oct–May Wed–Sun; tours only, times vary. Charge.

Like Mendips, John Lennon's childhood home, 20 Forthlin Road has been restored by the National Trust to look as close as possible as it would have done when Paul McCartney lived here from 1955 up until the early years of his fame in the early Sixties – right down to the vintage Ajax container on the kitchen shelf. The local tour guides will offer no room for negotiation on their assertion that this is the most significant house in rock 'n' roll history – Graceland, as little more than a glorified retirement home, apparently doesn't come close. The front room was where Paul and John wrote many of their early songs. On completing '*She Loves You*', the story goes, the excited pair ran through to the adjacent room to play it for Paul's father, Jim. McCartney Snr was encouraging, but, disapproving of encroaching Americanisms, suggested they replace 'Yeah, yeah yeah' with 'Yes, yes, yes' – the boys, probably wisely, stuck to their guns.

Shops

The Amorous Cat Gallery

MAP P.86

47 Lark Lane, L17. Bus: Lark Lane. http://
facebook.com/amcatgallery. Mon & Wed–
Sat 10.30am–5.30pm.

This art gallery is a showcase for a
rotating roster of eight local artists,
whose work depicts Merseyside life
from the glitzy to the mundane,
usually in cartoon form. Paintings
are for sale alongside prints and
greetings cards, and a piece of local
artwork is the perfect one-of-a-kind
gift.

Arta's Flowers

MAP P.86

24 Lark Lane, L17. Bus: Lark Lane. www.
artasflowers.co.uk. Tues–Sat 10am–6pm,
Sun 10am–5pm.

If you or anyone in your life has
a fondness for all things floral,
this gorgeous, tasteful Lark Lane
florist is the place to come for a gift
or souvenir. You'll find carefully
curated bunches of wildflowers,
paired for their colour and texture
combinations, alongside wreaths,
potpourri, button holes, pots and
more.

Freida Mo's

MAP P.86

33 Lark Lane, L17. Bus: Lark Lane. http://
facebook.com/FriedasLiverpool. Mon & Sun
11am–5pm, Tues–Sat until 6pm.

This bohemian boutique is worth a
visit just for the attached café, but
stick around to have a browse of its
vintage collection, which includes
boho chic dresses, blouses and
jackets alongside some rare vinyls,
much of them from the Sixties and
Seventies.

Gasp

MAP P.86

4 Lucerne St, L17. Bus: Lark Lane. 0151
222 1568. Thurs–Sun 11am–5pm.

Just off Lark Lane on Lucerne
Street, Gasp is no more than a
garage from the outside, but within

is a fantastically eclectic collection
of vintage homeware, clothing
and artwork. Whether you're after
a retro radio, enamel jugs and
lampshades, vintage guidebooks
and travel posters, or high-quality
Ercol furniture, this is the place to
find it.

Larks

MAP P.86

22 Lark Lane, L17. Bus: Lark Lane. http://
larksonline.co.uk. Mon–Fri 11am–5.30pm,
Sat 10am–5.30pm, Sun 11am–5pm.

If you're in the market for a
Liverpool souvenir that's a bit less
tacky than some of those found in
the city-centre's gift shops, Larks
does a lovely line in handmade
wooden keyrings and coasters,
Another Place sculpture miniature
metalwork, and Scouse dialect
tea towels. They also sell vintage
clothing and homeware.

Number 13

MAP P.86

13 Lark Lane, L17. Bus: Lark Lane. http://
facebook.com/number13larklane. Mon–Fri
11am–5.30pm, Sat 10am–5.30pm, Sun
11am–5pm.

Enter through Number 13's sky
blue doorway and you're greeted
with what at first glance looks like
a random and ramshackle pile of
jewellery, posters, bangles, candles
and assorted bohemian miscellanea.
Look closer and you might find
the perfect gift or souvenir, from
embroidered rugs and cushions to
books on neopaganism.

The Witch House

MAP P.86

49 Lark Lane, L17. Bus: Lark Lane. 0739
430 3441. Wed–Sun 11am–6pm.

Lovers of all things spooky and
esoteric will find plenty to divert
them at this emporium, which sells
everything the modern witch could
need: rubber insects in glass jars,
tarot cards, embroidered bags and
boots, and vintage clothing and
necklaces. Oh, and books of spells,
of course. There are occasional talks

Maranto's

and workshops, where you can learn how to put them into action.

Restaurants

Bistro Noir

MAP P.86
14 Lark Lane, L17. Bus: Lark Lane. http://bistronoir.co.uk. Wed–Thurs 4–8pm, Fri–Sat noon–9pm, Sun noon–7.30pm.
With its wooden tables and walls, gingham tablecloths and friendly family atmosphere, *Bistro Noir* is one of the cosiest spots on Lark Lane. The food is more eclectic than traditional French bistro fare – there's Jamaican goat curry, Malaysian laksa, and Greek salads on offer alongside juicy burgers and steaks. ££

Hafla Hafla

MAP P.86
73 Lark Lane, L17. Bus: Lark Lane. http://haflahafla.com. Mon–Fri noon–10pm, Sat 10am–10pm, Sun 10am–9pm.
This stylish spot, where vines seem to grow out of the redbrick walls, serves superb dishes inspired by Middle Eastern street food. That means spit-roasted chicken shawarmas, falafel kebabs, lamb and halloumi burgers, and a range of seriously indulgent loaded fries. There are loads of plant-based options too, so this is a good choice for vegans. £–££

Maranto's

MAP P.86
57 Lark Lane, L17. Bus: Lark Lane. http://marantoslarklane.co.uk. Daily noon–9.30pm.
Lark Lane's best and most beloved Italian restaurant has been run by the Italian American Maranto family since 1983. The space is homely and stylish, and the menu is a wide-ranging affair that covers traditional Italian classics as well as more contemporary dishes. Some highlights include the seafood risotto marinara, the minted lamb and the lamb Seville – chargrilled with garlic and oranges. There are also superb pizza and pasta dishes. ££

MeatMe

MAP P.86
20 Lark Lane, L17. Bus: Lark Lane. 0151 245 8310. Tues–Sun 4.30–10.30pm.
You'd be forgiven for thinking this Greek street food joint is a vegetarian's nightmare, given its name, but there are actually some good meat-free options on the menu, including halloumi wraps and vegan gyros fries. The mainstays are more classically carnivorous, including lamb souvlaki and pork gyros. £–££

The Old School House

MAP P.86
40 Lark Lane, L17. Bus: Lark Lane. www.theoldschoolhouse1889.com. Mon–Thurs noon–11.30pm, Fri noon–1am, Sat 10am–1am, Sun 10am–11.30pm.
Housed in a former school building dating back to 1889, this large and handsome gastro-pub serves delicious food throughout the day. Breakfast sees a selection of unpretentious dishes like smoked

salmon bagels and mushrooms on toast, before lunch and dinner take things international with things like chicken Penang curry and chimichurri cauliflower steak. ££

Woo Tan Scran

MAP P.86

109 Lark Lane, L17. Bus: Lark Lane. 0151 727 2890. Mon, Tues & Thurs–Sun 4–10pm.
Surely the best-named eatery in Liverpool is also the city's first-ever vegan chip shop (it had to be on Lark Lane). In keeping with the great Scouse tradition of the Chinese chippy, this ever-popular takeaway serves delicious Asian food, and it's all meat free – there's crispy jackfruit pancakes, sticky sesame nuggets and seitan 'meat' balls. Order a feast and take it to the park, if weather allows. ££

Yum Cha

MAP P.86

99 Lark Lane, L17. Bus: Lark Lane. http:// yumchaliverpool.co.uk. Mon–Thurs & Sun noon–9pm, Fri–Sat 12.30–9.30pm.
There's no shortage of fantastic Chinese restaurants in Liverpool, and now there's a superb dim sum place to add to the list in the form of Yum Cha. Served in traditional style in bamboo steamers, the dishes include classic Cantonese fare such as xia qui (prawn and sesame balls), char siu-filled bao, and siu mai (minced pork and prawn dumplings); from 2pm, a succulent array of roast meats, including duck, belly pork and chicken, become available too. ££

Bars

The Albert

MAP P.86

66 Lark Lane, L17. Bus: Lark Lane. 0151 726 9119. Mon–Thurs & Sun noon–11pm, Fri–Sat until midnight.
This is a Lark Lane institution which has been well kept to reflect its Victorian heritage. There's live big screen sport, occasional live music and a good range of draught beer. In keeping with the pub's vintage, there's also an extensive gin menu to choose from.

Fulwood Arms

MAP P.84

308 Aigburth Rd, L17. Bus: Mossley Hill Drive. http://facebook.com/fulwood.arms. Mon–Tues 4pm–midnight, Wed–Sat noon–midnight, Sun noon–11pm.
On the southern edge of Sefton Park, this friendly pub always has something going on, whether it's a quiz (Tuesdays), an open mic night (Thursdays) or football on the big screen. There's also good food, from chicken wings, fries and other bar bites to hearty Sunday roasts.

Keith's

MAP P.86

107 Lark Lane, L17. Bus: Lark Lane. http:// facebook.com/keithsfoodandwinebar. Mon–Thurs 9.30am–11pm, Fri–Sat until 2am.
There's a distinctly trad vibe about Keith's, from the wine-red exterior and vintage window sign to the live jazz which regularly soundtracks the evening's entertainment here. There's good food on offer throughout the day, but the place

Keith's

really comes to life at night – a lovely spot to linger over a glass of wine.

The Lodge

MAP P.86

33 Lark Lane, L17. Bus: Lark Lane. http://oldropewalks.co.uk/thelodgelarklane. Mon–Thurs & Sun noon–11pm, Fri–Sat until midnight.

Combining the aesthetic of a traditional city boozer with some hipsterish decor and wall art, *The Lodge* is Lark Lane down to a T. Monday evenings see live jazz, there's a quiz every Wednesday, and the pub hosts more live music every Sunday – the perfect accompaniment to a burger, fish and chips or home-baked pie.

Love & Rockets

MAP P.86

52 Lark Lane, L17. Bus: Lark Lane. http://loveandrocketslarklane.com. Daily 11am–late.

Proudly boasting no fewer than 30 varieties of whiskey and 40 of gin, you could spend quite some time exploring the offerings of this trendy bar. Vines and creepers are wreathed around old beer

Love & Rockets

kegs and bare brick walls, while hanging bulbs and neon cast the whole scene in a dimly atmospheric light; the soundtrack is taken care of by live jazz, blues and acoustic musicians.

Polidor 68

MAP P.86

89 Lark Lane, L17. Bus: Lark Lane. http://polidor68.com. Mon–Thurs 10.30am–10pm, Fri 10.30am–11pm, Sat 9.30am–11pm, Sun 9.30am–10pm.

Polidor 68 is inspired by Paris in 1968 – the year, apparently, when the city's underground bar scene exploded into life. Accordingly, there's a speakeasy feel to the place, and it's easy to miss, but once inside you'll be glad you made the effort to find it: the style evokes a Montmartre bolthole, there's a superb selection of wine and cocktails, and live jazz soundtracks four nights per week.

Cafés

Crosby Coffee

MAP P.86

62 Lark Lane, L17. Bus: Lark Lane. www.

crosbycoffee.co.uk. Mon–Fri 8am–5pm, Sat–Sun 9am–4pm.

With deliciously robust coffee roasted on-site, this is a small but cosy spot where a simple menu promises to fortify travellers after even the chilliest day browsing the boutiques of Lark Lane. The wide range of pasties, doughnuts and cakes make the perfect accompaniment. £

Freida Mo's

MAP P.86

33 Lark Lane, L17. Bus: Lark Lane. http://facebook.com/FriedasLiverpool. Mon & Sun 11am–5pm, Tues–Sat until 6pm.

As a bakery and café housed within a vintage boutique, *Freida Mo's* might just be the most Lark Lane place ever. Named after the owner's grandmothers, this is stylish in a bohemian way, with antique rugs underfoot and all manner of trinkets tottering on the shelves. There's great coffee and home-made cake, too. £

Milo Lounge

MAP P.86

90 Lark Lane, L17. Bus: Lark Lane. http://thelounges.co.uk/milo. Daily 9am–11pm.

With lime green wallpaper, brightly coloured tables and every wall covered with artwork and vintage mirrors, *Milo Lounge* is certainly characterful, but luckily there's substance to match the style. The huge menu includes sandwiches, burgers, and comfort food from across the globe from spicy bang bang chicken to American beef chilli, while there's good coffee, tea and cake. ££

Minna

MAP P.86

94 Lark Lane, L17. Bus: Lark Lane. www.facebook.com/minnaliverpool. Daily 9am–6pm.

A new addition to the Lark Lane scene, Minna opened in late 2022, with a fresh menu of brunch offerings to cater for the well-heeled Lark Lane crowd.

They include zingy salads made with roasted beetroot, hummus, rocket and orange, as well as hearty egg and sausage dishes, all beautifully presented and served in a stylishly appointed café setting. £–££

Pippin's Corner

MAP P.86

64 Lark Lane, L17. Bus: Lark Lane. http://facebook.com/pippinscornerliverpool. Mon 9am–5.30pm, Tues–Sun 9am–6pm.

In a cosy, dimly lit corner building, this pleasant café is the kind of place to escape to on a rainy day. Alongside espresso-style coffee and tea, there's a great range of breakfasts, from eggs Benedict to American-style pancakes, and lovely home-made pies and sandwiches. £–££

Rhubarb

MAP P.86

27 Lark Lane, L17. Bus: Lark Lane. 0151 728 9585. Tues–Fri 9.30am–6pm.

With half-cut barrels hanging on the walls, wrought iron light fixtures and a wood-panelled bar, *Rhubarb* has something of a saloon look in the front, giving way to a cosy purple-hued snug area in the back. The full English breakfasts here are particularly famous, with delicious veggie equivalents too. £–££

The Third

MAP P.86

13 Lark Lane, L17. Bus: Lark Lane. http://facebook.com/thethirdcafeliverpool. Daily 10am–5pm.

There's a Zen-like quality to *The Third*, with its peaceful atmosphere, minimalist decor and whitewashed furniture. The menu is vegetarian and vegan, with lovely breakfasts, healthy open sandwiches and huge, fresh salads; it does a lovely line in cosy winter warmers, like porridge with poached plums, and is perfectly placed for a cuppa after exploring Sefton Park. £

Around Liverpool

From unsettling modern art statues to quaint model villages and fiery football grounds, there's much to discover beyond Liverpool's city centre. Anfield is one of the world's most famous sports stadiums and will be high on the to-do list of any football fan, while the ground of their great rivals Everton, another of British football's most successful clubs, lies across the pretty Victorian expanse of Stanley Park. The coastline north of Liverpool, accessible within an hour by car or train, is home to some beautiful stretches of beach and woodland: at genteel Southport and Formby, and at Crosby, where Antony Gormley's starkly beautiful *Another Place* statues gaze eerily towards the sea.

Anfield

MAP P.98
Anfield Rd, L4. Bus: Liverpool FC. http://
liverpoolfc.com. Stadium tours daily
10am–3pm; schedule sometimes changes
for special events; check websites for
details. Charge.

Football gives music a run for its money as the great Liverpudlian obsession. The stadiums of the city's most famous clubs, Liverpool and Everton, can both be found in the northeast of the city, facing each other across Stanley Park. Anfield is the home of Liverpool Football Club, the city's most successful and one of the most successful in the country; Liverpool have won the European Cup six times, more than any other British team. At the time of writing they had also won 19 league titles, second only to their great rivals to the east, Manchester United, who had won 20. Liverpool's great heyday was during the 1970s and 1980s, since which time they have endured a relatively fallow period in terms of major trophies. The arrival of Jürgen Klopp in 2015, however, has ushered in a new period of success which delivered a first league title in 30 years in 2020.

Opened in 1884, Anfield is one of the oldest and most famous football grounds in the world. The on-site museum walks you through the club's long and storied history, from its beginnings as a 19th-century splinter club from Everton to the early glory years under Bob Paisley and through to the present day. For a more in-depth experience, the stadium tour takes

Goodison Park

Walking out onto the pitch on the Anfield tour

you behind the scenes, taking in views of the pitch from the top of the Main Stand, into the dressing rooms and press room, and you can emulate the greats by touching the iconic 'This is Anfield' sign before heading down the players' tunnel.

Stanley Park

MAP P.98

Walton Lane, L4. Bus: Florence St. http:// liverpool.gov.uk/leisure-parks-and-events. Daily 9.30am–9.30pm. Free.

To the north of Anfield is Stanley Park, a large, picturesque open space overshadowed by its association with football, but well worth a visit if you're in the area – even if you're only walking between the two great stadiums. Built in 1870, the park is home to an attractive fishing lake in the northwest corner. Nearby is the park's most famous feature, the Isla Gladstone Conservatory (daily 9.30am–3pm), a beautiful Victorian glasshouse which houses a café and the superb *Café in the Park* (see page 102).

Goodison Park

MAP P.98

Goodison Rd, L4. Bus: Bullens Rd. http:// evertonfc.com. Tour availability varies, but slots are 10am, 11.30am & 1pm. Charge.

On the northern edge of Stanley Park is Goodison Park, the home of Liverpool's great rivals, Everton. The older of the two clubs, Everton were initially the more successful, winning five league titles and two F.A. Cups before World War II. They enjoyed a brief resurgence in fortune during the 1960s and 1980s, winning a further four league championships during this time, but have been short on silverware since. As such, their museum is not quite as dazzling as Anfield's, but has just as interesting a story to tell – Everton are among the most successful clubs in British football, and have spent more seasons in the top flight than anyone else. Guided tours take you to the dressing room, down the tunnel and into the swanky hospitality lounges; the whole stadium is looking in great nick, having been spruced up recently as Everton's wealthy owners continue to splash the cash in an effort to get the club back to the top of the footballing tree.

Another Place figure on Crosby Beach

Shakespeare North Playhouse

MAP P.98
Prospero Place, Prescot,
L34. Metro: Prescot. https://
shakespearenorthplayhouse.co.uk.
The town of Prescot, around 12km
east of Liverpool city centre, is
the site of the new Shakespeare
North Playhouse, which opened
in July 2022. The complex,
comprising a 350-seat theatre,
outdoor performance garden
and visitor centre, promises to
complete England's 'Shakespearean
Triangle', with the other points
in London and Stratford-upon-
Avon. This is rather tenuous, given
that Shakespeare is not thought
to have ever visited this area – the
only link is his patronage by the
Earls of Derby, based at nearby
Knowsely Hall. That said, Prescot
is thought to have been the site of
the only purpose-built Elizabethan
theatre outside London, and the

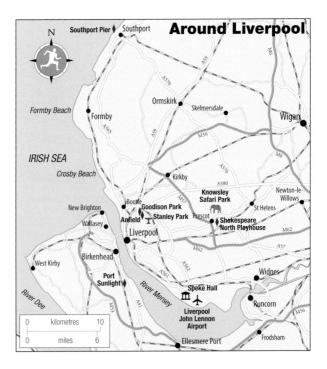

new construction looks set to be a stunner: a stylish contemporary exterior with an internal design inspired by Inigo Jones' Cockpit-in-Court theatre and the Globe's Sam Wanamaker Playhouse.

Crosby Beach

MAP P.98

Blundellsands Rd West, L23. Bus: Blundellsands & Crosby. Daily 24hr. Free.

Merseyside's most affecting art installation is not to be found in Liverpool's famous art galleries, but rather on a stretch of sandy beach 9km north of the city centre. Crosby Beach was an innocuous, if picturesque, spot until the arrival in 2005 of Antony Gormley's haunting *Another Place* installation, spread along more than two miles of the shore. An eerie set of a hundred life-size cast-iron statues, each cast from Gormley's own body, are buried at different levels in the sand, all gazing blankly out to sea and slowly becoming submerged as high tide rolls in. After similar exhibitions in Germany and Norway, the installation proved controversial upon its appearance on Merseyside,

and it was initially ruled that the sculptures would be removed before the council decreed that they could stay in 2007. To add to the sculptures' bleak beauty, nature is beginning to reclaim some of them as they grow thick with barnacles and algae.

To reach *Another Place*, it's a 20-minute train journey from Liverpool Central to Blundellsands and Crosby station, from where a ten-minute walk takes you down to the beach and the statues.

Formby

A further 8km north of Crosby, Formby cannot boast an Anthony Gormley of its own, but what it lacks in otherworldly artistic installations it more than makes up for in dramatic natural beauty. The beach here is a sweep of green-tufted sand dunes, the highest of which afford views of the Cumbrian mountains on a clear day. The dunes are an important habitat for the threatened natterjack toad, while the pine and poplar woods inland are a sanctuary for the red squirrel, whose population in the UK has

Formby beach

been severely threatened by the invasive grey squirrel.

The town itself is lovely, its high street home to some great restaurants and bars including the superb *Suay Pan* (see page 103). It's no coincidence that many of Merseyside's superrich footballers have made their home in Formby over the years.

Southport

Southport, 10km north of Formby, is another great beach escape within an hour's journey of Liverpool. With the rapid rise of Liverpool and Manchester during the Industrial Revolution came would-be holidaymakers with money to burn, and Southport rapidly became one of the most popular seaside resorts in the UK. Southport Beach is a pleasant stretch of golden sand dominated by Southport Pier (daily mid-July–Aug 10am–6pm, Sept–mid-July 11am–5pm; free), which juts out into the Irish Sea for

3,635ft – the second longest pier in the country behind Southend in Essex. Great coastal views can be had from the end of the pier; a vintage train (charge; every 30min) runs along its length if you don't fancy walking. There's also a café, traditional arcade machines, and, of course, a fish and chips restaurant.

Southport itself is an attractive town which wears its Victorian heritage elegantly. Lord Street, an arcaded boulevard flanked by gardens, brings to mind the prettier corners of Paris, and is said to have inspired them; no less a personage than Napoleon Bonaparte spent some time here in the mid-19th century. Highlights include the Botanic Gardens (Mon 7am–8pm, Tues–Sun 7.30am–8pm; free), opened in 1874 and home to a colourful array of flowers and a Victorian fernery, and the Atkinson Art Gallery & Library (http://theatkinson.co.uk; Mon–Sat 10am–4pm; free), which houses

The train on Southport Pier

a fantastic Egyptology collection. Perhaps surprisingly, Southport also claims to have the largest number of independent restaurants per square metre outside London; these include the superb *Kalash* (see page 103).

Port Sunlight

The Wirral village of Port Sunlight, 6km from central Liverpool, is more than just a lovely name. Built in the late 19th century to house the workers of the Lever Brothers soap company (the 'Sunlight' of the name, rather disappointingly, came from their popular detergent), this is the archetypal Victorian model village. Amazingly for a town of fewer than 1,500 people, Port Sunlight is home to a whopping 900 Grade II-listed buildings. Each of them is unique, but all are lovely; some are mock Tudor, while others were built with turrets in the Flemish style using bricks imported from Belgium. Still others have a belle époque feel. The village is an extremely relaxing place to walk around, but for more of an insight into its history visit the Port Sunlight Museum (Wed–Sun 10am–5pm; charge), which tells the story of the village's construction as well as its more recent history – Hulme Hall, just north of the train station, was where Ringo Starr made his first official performance with The Beatles in August 1962. Tickets to the museum also grant entry to Number 22, a cottage next door which has been renovated to appear as it would have done in the early 20th century when a Lever Brothers worker lived here with their family. Other highlights include the Lady Lever Art Gallery (Tues–Sun 10am–4pm; free), opened by William Lever in 1922 to house his vast art collection, which includes an unparalleled collection of Wedgwood jasperware and a treasure trove of Pre-Raphaelite masterpieces.

Speke Hall

Speke Hall

MAP P.98
The Walk, L24. Bus: DeHavilland Drive. http://nationaltrust.org.uk/speke-hall-garden-and-estate. Daily 10.30am–5pm. Charge.

One of northwest England's most beautiful buildings, Speke Hall was built between 1530 and 1598 as the family home of Sir William Norris, who was Member of Parliament for Liverpool in this period. The house is a classic Tudor wattle-and-daub construction set around a tree-shaded courtyard, with inner highlights including the impressive Great Hall, a masterpiece of Jacobean design, and the pokey priest hole – a reminder of the hardships Catholic priests were forced to endure during this period, and the risks that Catholic families like the Norrises took to protect them. Speke Hall was even fitted with an eavesdropper – a hole in the eaves of the house, so that the conversations of people at the front door could be spied upon. In addition to the house itself, Speke Hall is set in lovely wooded grounds where it's easy to spend an hour or two exploring.

Restaurants

Café in the Park

Stanley Park, L4. Bus: Anfield Rd. http://
theislagladstone.co.uk. Daily 9.30am–4pm.
In the elegant setting of Stanley
Park's Victorian Isla Gladstone
Conservatory, *Café in the Park*
has a contrastingly modern style
within, although many of the
menu offerings – haddock and
hand-cut chips, Welsh rarebit, BLT
sandwiches – are reassuringly trad.
A lovely place to stop by for lunch
during a visit to Stanley Park or one
of the football stadiums. £

Don Luigi

31 Church Rd, L37. Bus: Church Rd.
http://donluigirestaurant.co.uk. Tues–Fri
3.45–9pm, Sat 1–9pm, Sun 2–8pm.
Formby's best-loved Italian
restaurant is a big, convivial space,
with dining space across two floors
and an outside terrace. The menu
includes not only superb pizza and
pasta dishes, but a wide range of
meat and fish recipes like peppered
pork and salmon *fagiolini*. From
Wed–Sat, 4–6pm, 'happy hour'
means cut-price pizzas or a popular
'pizza and a glass of wine' deal –
bargain. £–££

Fat Italian

70 Coronation Rd, L23. Bus: Harrington
Rd. http://fatitalian.co.uk. Mon–Sat 4pm–
midnight, Sun noon–midnight.
Dimly lit and with a cosy
atmosphere that brings to mind
an authentic country trattoria, the
Fat Italian does a superb line in
hearty, homestyle Italian cooking.
Alongside superb pizza and pasta,
there's chargrilled swordfish steak,
Sicilian roast beef, and slow-roasted
belly pork. In true Merseyside style,
there's also a menu section devoted
to salt and pepper dishes, using a
seasoning mix brought to Liverpool
by Chinese sailors. ££

The Hungry Monk

18 Cambridge Arcade, PR8. Bus: Lord St.
www.thehungrymonk.co.uk. Wed–Sun
noon–late.
Hearty, traditional dishes – much
like those which, presumably,
would once have bene enjoyed
by a hungry monk – are the
order of the day at this likeable
restaurant. Dishes are hearty and
unpretentious, and portions are

Don Luigi's antipasti

Isla Gladstone Conservatory in Stanley Park

large – offerings include Welsh rarebit on 'doorstop toast' and jacket potatoes stuffed with ham and cheese, alongside more cosmopolitan pizzas and nachos, and a wide range of beers. £–££

Kalash Divine

1 Lord St, PR8. Bus: Lord St. http://kalash.co.uk. Wed–Sat 6–10pm.

As heavenly as its name suggests is Southport's finest and best-loved Indian restaurant, which sees subcontinental dishes – including hearty biryanis, creamy butter chicken, and rich fish curries – served with artistry in a refined environment. The menu really comes into its own with the grilled meat dishes; try the barrah champ (marinated, charcoal-grilled rack of lamb). ££

Suay Pan

3 School Lane, L37. Bus: School Lane. http://suayformby.co.uk. Tues–Sun noon–10pm.

Can't decide whether you fancy Thai, Indian, Malaysian or Chinese for dinner? There's no need to choose at *Suay Pan*, a superb pan-Asian restaurant which delivers

an extremely cosmopolitan menu without ever skipping a beat. Highlights include the Vietnamese lamb cutlets, Penang sea bass and pad Thai. ££

Tree House

60 Coronation Rd, L23. Bus: Harrington Rd. http://treehousecrosby.co.uk. Mon–Thurs noon–9pm, Fri–Sat noon–9.30pm, Sun 2–8pm.

Living up to its name with a green-fingered decor that sees vines crawling up the walls and ceilings, hung with flowers and prettily intertwined with fairy lights, the *Tree House* is beloved in Crosby for its friendly atmosphere and down-to-earth menu of international favourites, from scouse pie to fajitas via racks of ribs and roast chicken. Stick around for the home-made chocolate brownies. ££

Bars

Beer Station

3 Victoria Buildings, L37. Metro: Freshfield. www.facebook.com/beerstationformby. Mon–Thurs 3–9pm, Fri 2–10pm, Sat noon–10pm, Sun 2–9pm.

The Lakeside Inn

Just the place to aim for at the end of a long Formby Beach walk, the *Beer Station* is run by Ian and Keir, a father and son team passionate about all things brewed and hoppy. An ever-changing line-up of bottled and cask beers come courtesy of local producers, enjoyed in a cosy café-style environment.

The Grasshopper

70 Sandon Rd, PR8. Bus: Sandon Rd. http://twitter.com/the_grasshopper. Mon–Fri 5–10pm, Sat–Sun noon–10.30pm.
With its high wall-facing seats, bookshelves and exposed brick walls, *The Grasshopper* feels more like a coffee bar than a British pub. It serves a superb selection of beers and ciders, most of them from local producers, and has been acclaimed as one of the finest 'micropubs' in the UK.

Lakeside Inn Southport

Marine Lake Promenade, PR9. Bus: Knowesly Rd. http://facebook.com/SueLakesideInn. Mon–Sat noon–11pm, Sun noon–10.30pm.
Certified as Britain's smallest pub, the *Lakeside Inn* – overlooking Southport's Marine Lake – is indeed tiny, though thanks to wall-hugging bench seats and some creative use of mirrors, it doesn't feel as cramped as you might imagine. There's a good wine list, and the handmade pork pies are the house speciality.

The Sandon

166–182 Oakfield Rd, L4. Bus: Houlding St. http://thesandon.com. Daily 11am–11pm.
Something of a pre-match institution for Liverpool fans, *The Sandon* was the first Masonic lodge in Liverpool and was actually once the headquarters of Everton FC – although you'd be ill-advised to wear a Toffees jersey in here these days. The pub is worth a visit before or after a stadium tour, but it gets extremely busy around match times.

Scotch Piper

Southport Rd, Lydiate, L31. Bus: Station Rd. http://scotchpiper.com. Mon–Thurs & Sun 9am–11pm, Fri–Sat until midnight.
The oldest pub in Lancashire, the *Scotch Piper* in Lydiate dates way back to 1320 – and having retained its lovely wooden beams, thatched roof and log fires, it looks it, too. With live music every weekend and weekly classic car and motorbike meets, there's always something going on, and any day of the week it's a lovely spot to curl up with a pint of good beer in front of the log fire.

Tap and Bottles

19a Cambridge Walks, PR8. Bus: Lord St. www.facebook.com/tapandbottles. Mon–Thurs noon–11pm, Fri–Sat until midnight, Sun until 10.30pm.
Another bastion of Southport's thriving independent beer scene, this stylish bar showcases the best new brews from across the country and beyond. Every June sees the bar put on its own festival in Cambridge Arcade, Southport Beer Street, with more than 80 beers for punters to try.

The Victoria

42 Stanley Terrace, PR9. Bus: Promenade. http://victoriasouthport.co.uk. Mon–Thurs & Sun noon–midnight, Fri–Sat until 1am.
While the outdoor beer terrace is always overflowing in the summer months, *The Victoria* is a good bet throughout the year: a traditional

pub on Southport's promenade overlooking Marine Lake. Living up to its name, the pub has retained the decor of Southport's Victorian heyday, and has a nice convivial atmosphere.

Cafés

Andy's Snack Bar

1 Garricks Parade, PR8. Metro: Southport. www.facebook.com/andyssnackbar. Mon–Sat 7am–2.30pm.

Those with a taste for hearty, cheap and cheerful British food will love *Andy's Snack Bar*. Meat pies are slathered with gravy and served with chips and mushy peas, the full English breakfasts spill over the sides of the plate and come with mountains of buttered toast, and strong tea is served in robust mugs, not dainty teacups. £

The Azul Monkey

157 College Rd, L23. Metro: Blundellsands & Crosby. http://azulmonkey.co.uk. Tues–Sun 10am–4pm.

This curiously named café serves superb coffee and hearty breakfasts, just the thing for refuelling after a windswept winter walk on the beach. The 'mighty monkey breakfast' is a good place to start, featuring Stornaway black pudding, vine tomatoes, bacon, sausages and the rest, while the Biscoff pancakes are an alternative for those with a sweet tooth. £–££

Geee's Coffee

52 Brows Ln, L37. Metro: Freshfield. 07773 487249. Tues–Sun 9.30am–3.30pm.

The kind of café that small British towns do best, Geee's is friendly, unpretentious, and does a great line in classic breakfast dishes, from traditional full English offerings to the ever-fashionable eggs and avocado on toast. The cakes and pastries are hard to turn down, too. £

A Great Little Place

The Atkinson, Lord St, PR8. Metro: Southport. http://agreatlittleplace.org. Mon–Sat 10am–4pm.

Now in a new home in the fantastic Atkinson Art Gallery, this café does superb coffee and a small but well-presented menu of country dishes like baked Lancashire cheese flan, Cumberland sausage sandwiches, and pea and basil soup. Profits go towards improving the lives of people with autism. £

The Kitchen

4 Chapel Alley, L37. Bus: Formby Village. www.facebook.com/TheKitchenFormby. Mon–Sat 8.30am–4.30pm, closed Wed.

No-frills café perfect for warming up after a walk on the beach. The coffee, tea and hot chocolate are all good, and there's a wide range of cakes and pastries to accompany them. For something substantial, try the all-day breakfasts, which come in meat and veggie form, home-made soups, or paninis. £

Vintage Tea Room

4 Botanic Rd, PR9. Bus: Off Botanic Rd. http://facebook.com/VintageTeaRoom1. Mon–Sat 9.30am–4pm.

The brick-effect wallpaper makes you question this tearoom's 'vintage' credentials, but there's no doubting the quality of the offerings here. The sandwiches are big and hearty, made with fresh local ingredients, while the cakes and pastries on offer are just as delicious. The main event is the superb afternoon tea, but there's also good coffee available. £

The Wagging Tail

62 Botanic Rd, PR9. Bus: Off Botanic Rd. http://thewaggingtail.org. Wed–Sun 10am–3pm.

Dogs, owners and dog lovers alike will feel at home at this friendly 'hound and human café', where the dog menu – featuring pupcakes, pupcorn and dog beer – is as extensive as the human one. The latter includes top coffee, afternoon tea and home-made cakes, as well as sandwiches and all-day breakfasts. £

Further Afield

Whether you're looking to delve into the world-class culture of the other great cities of the north, or explore some of the most spectacular wildernesses in Great Britain, you're spoilt for choice when it comes to day trips from Liverpool. Manchester's elegant core of converted warehouses and glass skyscrapers is a far cry from the smoke-covered sprawl George Orwell once described as "the belly and guts of the nation", and today includes some of the region's best bars, restaurants and museums. Chester is home to a glorious ring of medieval and Roman walls encircling a kernel of Tudor and Victorian buildings, all overhanging eaves, mini-courtyards and narrow cobbled lanes. To the east, the Peak District boasts some of the most spectacular landscapes in England, the country's stereotypical rolling hills sharpened into dramatic peaks as if lifted skyward by invisible hooks, while to the north, the Lakes, along with their surrounding forests and fells, have long inspired painters and poets.

Manchester

Locked in a perpetual battle with Birmingham for the title of the United Kingdom's second city, Manchester, much like Liverpool, is defined by three things: music, industry and football. Also like Liverpool, Manchester underwent a decline in the decades following World War II before enjoying a renaissance in the 1990s, an economic upturn accompanied by a wave of good feeling ushered in by the success of Manchester United Football Club and the swagger of bands like Oasis, the Stone Roses and the Happy Mondays. Today, Manchester remains one of the country's most vibrant cities, with the old industrial mills and Georgian terraces of Ancoats and the Northern Quarter repurposed as bohemian cafés, bars and music venues. Just 40 minutes by train from Lime Street, Manchester is easy to visit on a day trip from Liverpool, though you may well be tempted to stay for longer.

Manchester Art Gallery

Mosley St, M2. http://manchesterartgallery. org. Tues–Sun 10am–5pm, first Wed of the month until 9pm. Free.

Manchester Art Gallery, as well as attracting big-name exhibitions by contemporary artists, holds an invigorating collection of eighteenth- and nineteenth-century art. Spread across Floor 1, these works are divided by theme – Face and Place, Natural Forces and so on – rather than by artist (or indeed school of artists), which makes it difficult to appreciate the strength of the collection, especially when it comes to its forte, the Pre-Raphaelites. There's much else – views of Victorian Manchester, a Turner or two, a pair of Gainsboroughs and Stubbs's famous *Cheetah and Stag with Two Indians* to name but a few. Floor 2

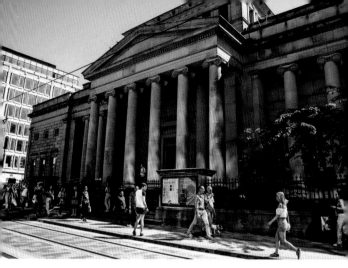

Manchester Art Gallery

features temporary exhibitions and crafts, while the Ground Floor's Manchester Gallery is devoted to a visual history of the city. The Clore Art Studio is fun for kids.

Museum of Science and Industry

Liverpool Rd, M3. Metro: Deansgate-Castlefield. http://scienceandindustrymuseum.org.uk. Daily 10am–5pm. Free.

One of the most impressive museums of its type in the country, the Museum of Science and Industry mixes technological displays and blockbuster exhibitions with trenchant analysis of the social impact of industrialization. Key points of interest include the Power Hall, which trumpets the region's remarkable technological contribution to the Industrial Revolution by means of a hall full of steam engines, some of which are fired up daily. There's more steam in the shape of a working replica of Robert Stephenson's *Planet*, whose original design was based on the Rocket, the work of Robert's father George. The 1830 Warehouse features a sound and light show that delves into the history of the city's

immense warehouses, and the Air and Space Hall, which barely touches on Manchester at all, features vintage planes, cutaway engines and space exploration displays.

People's History Museum

Left Bank, Spinningfields, M3. Metro: Deansgate-Castlefield. http://phm.org.uk. Daily except Tues 10am–5pm, second Thurs of the month until 8pm. Free.

The superb People's History Museum explores Britain's rich history of radicalism and the struggles of marginalized people to acquire rights and extend suffrage – ideas that developed out of the workers' associations and religious movements of the industrial city and which helped to shape the modern world. Housed in a former pump house and an ultramodern, four-storey extension, the galleries use interactive displays – including coffins and top hats – to trace a compelling narrative from the Peterloo Massacre of 1819 onwards. As the gallery shows, this moment became the catalyst for agitation that led to the 1832 Reform Act, and subsequent rise of the egalitarian Chartist movement; the museum played a big part

John Rylands Library

of football and pop music, and include the finest collection of trade union banners in the country.

John Rylands Library

150 Deansgate, M3. www.library.manchester.ac.uk/rylands. Mon–Sun noon–5pm, Tues–Sat 10am–5pm. Free.

Nestling between Spinningfields and the north end of Deansgate, John Rylands Library is the city's supreme example of Victorian Gothic – notwithstanding the presence of an unbecoming modern entrance wing. The architect who won the original commission, Basil Champneys, opted for a cloistered neo-Gothicism of narrow stone corridors, delicately crafted stonework, stained-glass windows and burnished wooden panelling. The library, which has survived in superb condition, now houses specialist collections of rare books and manuscripts. Be sure to visit the Rylands Gallery, where some

in the 2019 two-hundred-year anniversary. The galleries go on to explore the struggle for female suffrage, the Communist party in Britain, Oswald Mosley's fascists, and the working-class origins

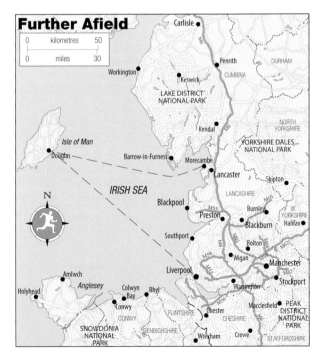

of the collection's rarest documents are on display, including the St John Fragment. Thought to date to 200 AD, making it the oldest piece of New Testament writing in existence, this Greek papyrus fragment lay in the library's archive undiscovered for decades until it was unearthed in the 1930s.

Chester

Though it cannot boast the industrial might, pop cultural significance or urban buzz of Liverpool, Chester, 25km to the south, is one of the most historic cities in England and must be one of the prettiest. It was founded by the Romans in AD 79 as Deva Victrix, and vestiges of this era remain in the city's Roman ruins; the superb Grosvenor Museum tells the story of Chester from this era to the present day.

Chester Cathedral

9 Abbey Square, CH1. http://chestercathedral.com. Mon–Sat 9.30am–6pm, Sun 9.30am–5pm. Free, but donation suggested. Cathedral at Height tours are regular, but check website for specific times; 1hr. Charge.

Chester's cathedral is a much-modified red sandstone structure dating back to the Norman era. The nave, with its massive medieval pillars, is suitably imposing, and on one side it sports a splendid sequence of Victorian Pre-Raphaelite mosaic panels that illustrate Old Testament stories in melodramatic style. Close by, the north transept is the oldest and most Norman part of the church – hence the round-headed arch and arcade – and the adjoining choir holds an intricately carved set of fourteenth-century choir stalls with some especially beastly misericords. The atmospheric East Cloister leads to a gorgeously tranquil garden.

The Cathedral at Height tour, an enjoyable rootle around the building's previously hidden spaces, takes you up onto the roof for panoramic views over five counties – you'll even spot Liverpool's cathedrals.

Grosvenor Museum

27 Grosvenor St, CH1. http://grosvenormuseum.westcheshiremuseums.co.uk. Mon–Sat 10.30am–5pm, Sun 1–4pm. Free; donation suggested.

Scores of sculpted tomb panels and engraved headstones once propped up the wall to either side of the Water Tower, evidence of some nervous repair work undertaken when the Roman Empire was in retreat. Much of this stonework was retrieved by the Victorians and is now on display at the Grosvenor Museum, which also has interesting background displays on the Roman Empire in general, and Roman Chester in particular. At the rear of the museum is 20 Castle Street, a period house with nine rooms tricked out to represent domestic scenes from 1680 to 1925.

The Roman Gardens and Amphitheatre

Daily 9am–6pm. Free.

Immediately to the east of one of the old city gates, Newgate, a

The pretty centre of Chester

Hiking in the snow near Kinder Scout

footpath leads into the Roman Gardens (open access), where a miscellany of Roman stonework – odd bits of pillar, coping stones and incidental statuary – is on display. Footsteps away, along Little St John Street, is the shallow, partly excavated bowl that marks the site of the Roman Amphitheatre (open access); it is estimated to have held seven thousand spectators, making it the largest amphitheatre in Britain, but frankly it's not much to look at today.

Peak District

Beginning around 65km east of central Liverpool, the Peak District (http://peakdistrict.gov.uk) was the first designated national park in England and remains one of the great British wildernesses. The central and southern section of the park, the White Peak, is a limestone plateau between 270m and 340m above sea level, all undulating hills and verdant valleys. To the north, the Dark Peak is wilder, higher – its highest point, Kinder Scout, reaching 636m – and more striking, its black granite rock forming jagged spires and deep depressions filled with thick peat bogs. Accessible walks in the Peak District include the popular Mam Tor – also known by the evocative alternative name Shivering Mountain for its frequent shale landslips – and the Cromford Mill and Village Route. The latter takes in the famous eighteenth-century Arkwright Mill, the world's first water-powered cotton mill, and the High Peak Trail, a scenic route along a former industrial railway.

Chatsworth House

Bakewell, DE45. http://chatsworth.org. Daily 11am–5pm; 10am–4pm during winter. Charge.
On the eastern edge of the Peak District sits Chatsworth House, one of the country's most famous stately homes. Chatsworth is the ancestral home of the Duke and Duchess of Devonshire, and was built from 1687–1708 in grand Baroque style. Highlights of the house include the Painted Hall, its ceiling adorned with beautiful murals, and the grand State Drawing Room, built to be quite literally fit for a king. Besides the stunning artistry of the building itself, Chatsworth houses a considerable collection of artworks, including many by the

Old Masters and contemporary art in the North Sketch Gallery. The 105-acre grounds, meanwhile, with their ponds, waterfalls, mazes and grottoes, are a world unto themselves.

Lake District

Alongside the Peaks, the Lake District – around 90km north of Liverpool – is the jewel in northern England's crown. A vast expanse of lakes, forests and hills, it's no wonder that the landscapes in these parts were such a source of inspiration to William Wordsworth, Samuel Taylor Coleridge, and their fellow 19th-century Lake Poets. Owing to the Lakes's historic and literary associations, there is more in the way of cultural attractions here than in the Peaks, although many come here purely for the hiking.

Windermere

Lakeland's most famous sight is Windermere, the largest lake in England. A ribbon lake that sprawls for almost 17km, its shores are surrounded by forested hills, the setting for some fantastic walking routes. Those in pursuit of a more leisurely stroll should try one of the 'miles without stiles' routes, such as the 2km Bowness to Cockshott Point or the 9km Western Shore route, which affords beautiful views north to the Troutbeck Hills on a clear day. Further from the lakeshore, the lovely Greenwood Trails amble through old-growth forests between quaint villages like Satterthwaite and Rusland. The pretty church in Rusland is the resting place of British author Arthur Ransome, whose Swallows and Amazons book series details children's adventures in the Lakes and has been credited with kickstarting the popularity of the Windermere area as a tourist destination.

Blackwell

Rydal, LA22. http://rydalmount.co.uk. Nov–Feb daily 10.30am–4pm, March–Oct until 5pm. Charge.

It's hard to disagree with Blackwell's claim to be the 'most beautiful house in the Lakes'. Built in 1901 as a holiday home by the wealthy Manchester brewer Sir Edward Holt, the house was designed by the famous architect Baillie Scott and is a magnificent example of the Arts and Crafts style, typified by steep roofs and a basis in earthy, vernacular styles rather than cold classicism. Today the house remains as beautiful as it ever was. Highlights include the Dining Room, notable for its blue-and-white striped fireplace and antique hessian wall hanging; the simple but charming Yellow Bedroom, which commands spectacular views over Windermere; and the Main Hall, its wooden ceiling and wall beams having a Tudor feel.

Rydal Mount House and Gardens

Rydal, LA22. http://rydalmount.co.uk. Apr–Oct daily 9.30am–5pm, Nov–March Wed–Sun 11am–4pm. Charge.

In between the town of Ambleside and the village of Grasmere and overlooking Lake Windermere, Rydal Mount was the family home of William Wordsworth from 1813 to 1850, the year of his death. The house, a lovely whitewashed building dating from the 16th century, is still owned by the Wordsworth family and has been appointed to look much as it would have done when the poet lived here, with its antique wooden furniture, elegantly fading wooden rugs, and airy living room. The property's nicest feature, though, is the five acres of landscaped gardens, designed by Wordsworth himself – he was known to say that it was the grounds, rather than the study within the house, that served as his office.

ACCOMMODATION

The Presidential Suite at the DoubleTree by Hilton Hotel & Spa

Accommodation

Liverpool's accommodation scene is diverse and ever-expanding, with a fine array of places to lay your head no matter what your budget. There are gorgeous townhouse hotels nestled in Liverpool's Georgian terraces, Victorian villas repurposed into cosy B&Bs, sleek modern boutiques, and vast hotels in the atmospheric surroundings of old warehouses, which evoke the money and might of Liverpool's golden industrial age. While there is no end of luxury to be enjoyed, Liverpool is also friendly to travellers on a shoestring, and there are great hostels and budget hotels which don't have to mean a compromise on location. These entry-level hotel rooms start at as little as £15 for a dorm bed in high season, while rooms in the city's more expensive hotels can easily cost upwards of £300.

St George's Quarter

RADISSON RED MAP P.26. Lime St, L1. Metro: Lime St. http://radissonhotels. com. Part of Radisson's design-focused RED portfolio, this arty hotel opened in December 2022 in a magnificent building dating back to 1871 which once served as a railway hotel for passengers at nearby Lime Street. Long derelict, it's been renovated to its Victorian grandeur and updated with pop-art touches of colour and style. Rooms have a sleek, modern look and a dark colour palette, and the Stoke Restaurant serves lovely British and European food. **££–£££**

THE SHANKLY MAP P.26. 60 Victoria St, L1. Metro: Lime St. http://shanklyhotel. com. Named, themed and decorated in honour of Liverpool institution Bill Shankly, the legendary manager of Liverpool FC, The Shankly is a hotel for football fanatics. Walls are adorned with inspirational quotes from the great man, and guestrooms have a classic look which wouldn't have been out of place in his 1950s heyday – with the benefit of modern features like whirlpool bathtubs. The Bastion Bar & Restaurant specialises in classic British dishes – try the pork belly with cauliflower purée. **££**

Waterfront

30 JAMES STREET MAP P.36. 30 James St, L2. Bus: James St. http://30jamesstreetliverpool.co.uk. Occupying the former headquarters of the White Star Line company, owners of the doomed *Titanic*, this plush hotel evokes the early 20th-century glamour of the world's most famous cruise liner. Guestrooms are decked out like luxurious wooden cabins, while opulent suites on the London and New York floors are designed in the style of those cities' luxury hotels in times past. The *Carpathia* restaurant serves classic cuisine from the same era, while the rooftop champagne bar of the same name (see page 47) offers spectacular views over the city. **££–£££**

CAMPANILE MAP P.36. Chaloner St, L3. Bus: Blundell St. http://campanile.com. A decent bed and breakfast perfectly placed for exploring the trendy bars and cafés of the bohemian Baltic Triangle, *Campanile* has the feel of an American motel. Rooms are basic but comfortable, with TV and chargeable wi-fi, and the breakfast offers a good selection of Continental and cooked options. Throughout the day there's a range of sandwiches and light bites available at the restaurant. Prices are almost halved outside of peak season. **£–££**

MALMAISON MAP P.36. 7 William Jessop Way, L3. Bus: Gibraltar Row. http://malmaison.com. Enjoying pride of place on Princes Dock, the *Malmaison* is a stylish, modern hotel. Rooms are cheerfully decorated, with arty maps of Liverpool adorning the walls, big comfy beds, and sleek colour schemes of grey and black with a dash of purple. The *Chez Mal* brasserie serves hearty British dishes like cottage pie and bangers and mash, while the stylish velvet sofas of the bar are perfect for enjoying a nightcap. **££**

PULLMAN MAP P.36. King's Dock, L3. Bus: Halftide Wharf. http://pullman. accor.com. Right next to the ACC Liverpool exhibition centre, the *Pullman* is a stylish four-star in a modern building on the King's Dock. Rooms combine colourful contemporary furniture with feature walls bearing moody black-and-white shots of Liverpool's skyline, as well as more historic shots from the dock's industrial past. *Wheeler's Oyster Bar* is a wonderful spot for a seafood dinner or a cocktail. **££**

TITANIC MAP P.36. Stanley Dock, L3. Bus: Dublin St. http://titanichotelliverpool. com. *Titanic* by name, titanic by nature, this vast hotel occupies a former warehouse building on the Stanley Dock. Rooms have retained striking period features, like exposed brick walls and vast metal columns and girders, but have been tastefully decorated with vintage posters with cruise liners from Liverpool's shipping era. There's a sleek spa and gym in the basement, while *Stanley's* serves superb breakfasts and a good range of Italian and British food. **££–£££**

YHA ALBERT DOCK MAP P.36. 25 Tabley St, L1. Bus: Queens Wharf. http://yha.org. uk. A stone's throw from the Albert Dock, this professionally-run hostel is a great budget choice for backpackers looking to explore Liverpool. The spacious dorms, sleeping two to eight, have wooden floors and lime green bunks, while the cheerfully decorated common areas have TVs and brightly coloured sofas where you can get to know your fellow travellers. At the *Liver Lounge & Café*, there's a good range of pizzas, burgers and paninis, with breakfast also available in the morning. Dorms **£**

Cavern Quarter

ALOFT LIVERPOOL MAP P.52. Central Buildings, North John St, L2. Bus: North John St. http://marriott.com. Housed in the beautiful Grade II-listed Royal Insurance Building, *Aloft* is a much more modern proposition inside, with rooms decked out in grey and dark wood and stylized artworks depicting the Liverpool skyline on the walls. The *NYL Restaurant* (see page 56) is more traditionally elegant and serves up decent New York-inspired food, while the hotel also has a well-equipped gym open 24 hours, seven days a week. **££**

DOUBLETREE BY HILTON HOTEL & SPA MAP P.52. 6 Sir Thomas St, L1. Metro: Moorfields. http://doubletree3.hilton.com. It's the building that makes this four-star remarkable: a handsome nineteenth-century corner property built in the Corinthian style, which has recently been restored to its former glory. That means lounge areas with vintage leather sofas, parquet floors and bookshelves and wall arches carved from rich dark wood, while the bar, which has a slightly more mid-century feel, is particularly stylish. Some of the rooms also boast period features like wooden wall panels, but for the most part they have a rather anonymous, modern feel. **££–£££**

HARD DAY'S NIGHT MAP P.52. Central Buildings, North John St, L2. Metro: James St. http://harddaysnighthotel.com. Perhaps surprisingly, this claims to be the world's only Beatles-themed hotel. It certainly lives up to the name: Beatles smile (or sing) down at you from the walls of all the guestrooms, while the ultra-luxe Lennon Suite even features its own white baby grand piano, so you can re-enact the *Imagine* video if you are so inclined. Beneath the surface, though, this is just a well-run, comfortable four-star, with spacious, modern rooms, bland en-suite bathrooms, and decent British food at

Blakes Restaurant (see page 55). **£££**

HEYWOOD HOUSE MAP P.52. 11 Fenwick St, L2. Metro: James St. http://heywoodhousehotel.co.uk. In a convenient location right next to James Street train station, this is a comfortable hotel, with spacious guestrooms that are traditional without being fusty, with the occasional column or window detail that betrays the building's heritage as a Georgian-era bank. Adjacent to the hotel is the stylish *Alchemist* bar, where hearty breakfasts are on offer for hotel guests. **££**

THE SIR THOMAS MAP P.52. 24 Sir Thomas St, L1. Bus: Cumberland St. http://thesirthomas.co.uk. The venerable name is matched by the atmosphere in this nineteenth-century building, although the rooms are a bit gloomy and have rather old-fashioned decor and wallpaper disconcertingly reminiscent of gold lamé. That said, they're comfortable and good value, and all have TV, wi-fi and tea and coffee facilities. The brasserie downstairs does good breakfasts, Sunday roasts and afternoon tea. **££**

YHA LIVERPOOL CENTRAL MAP P.52. Kansas Building, Mathew St, L2. Bus: The Metquarter. http://yha.org.uk. The ever-reliable *YHA* is a sociable place to stay, with a colourfully painted living area and kitchen where you can hang out with fellow travellers. The grandly-named 'suites' are in fact six-bed dorms, albeit each boasting their own lounge area with TV; they also have spacious lockers, but no curtains on the bunks, which can be a downside for people who value their privacy. Decent value doubles are also available. **£**

Z HOTEL MAP P.52. 2 North John St, L2. Metro: Moorfields. http://thezhotels.com/hotels/Liverpool. The cheapest rooms at this modern hotel are small – you can virtually roll out of bed into the shower – and have no windows, but offer decent value and are clean and comfortable. With light wood headboards, grey curtains and not much in the way of additional wall art, even the bigger rooms are unremarkable, but all have wi-fi and HD cable TV, and are

hard to beat for price in this touristy part of town. **£–££**

Ropewalks

ARTHOUSE HOTEL MAP P.62. 42 Seel St, L1. Metro: Liverpool Central. http://arthousehotelliverpool.co.uk. Themed, as the name suggests, around the worlds of art and cinema, *Arthouse* promises a memorable stay. Those of a flamboyant disposition will enjoy the black velvet and paisley stylings of the Rocky Horror room, while the Psycho room is thankfully rather more luxurious than the Bates Motel – those possessed of a vivid imagination may still want to stay vigilant in the shower, however. **££**

EPIC SEEL STREET HOTEL MAP P.62. 42 Seel Street, L1. Metro: Liverpool Central. http://epichotels.co.uk. Arty hotel with a good range of rooms, from the entry-level Cinema Suites, which are small but stylish and adorned with movie posters, to the optimistically named Wow! Suite, which is bigger than the latter but by no means huge and has a balcony. *Mason's* restaurant serves superb breakfasts, burgers and steaks. **££**

HATTERS HOSTEL MAP P.62. 56–60 Mount Pleasant, L3. Bus: Rodney St. http://hattershostels.com. Stylishly decorated hostel with a selection of spacious private rooms and four- to 14-bed dorms. The latter have privacy curtains, reading lights and nice wood-effect bunks, while privates are decked out in pastel shades and have wooden floors and furniture. Cheap breakfasts are on offer downstairs (£5), which are good value and offer a decent cooked selection. **£**

LOCK & KEY MAP P.62. 15–17 Duke St, L1. Metro: Liverpool Central. http://lockandkeyhotels.com. This lovely boutique hotel is housed in a beautiful Georgian townhouse. The rooms retain lovely period features like antique cast iron radiators, but have a stylishly modern feel thanks to a sleek dark colour scheme and stylized floral wall decor. The restaurant of the same name downstairs does one of the best hotel breakfasts in town. **££–£££**

OYO GRAND CENTRAL MAP P.62. 35 Renshaw St, L1. Metro: Liverpool Central. http://oyorooms.com. In the beautiful Grand Central Hall – a redbrick 1905 building in the Art Nouveau style – this modern chain hotel can't live up to the exterior, but is perfectly passable. The rooms have brightly painted feature walls, wooden floors and desks; single rooms are also available. **££–£££**

PRINTWORKS MAP P.62. 13 Renshaw St, L1. Bus: Liverpool Central. http://printworksliverpool.com. While it's not a patch on the heritage hotels it seeks to mimic – guestrooms have brick- and wood-effect wallpaper, in lieu of the real thing – *Printworks* lives up to its name in that respect and is nevertheless a good value, comfortable and well-run option close to Ropewalks and the Georgian Quarter. The bar/restaurant downstairs does decent breakfasts, and has drinks, snacks and light meals available throughout the day. **£**

THE RESIDENT MAP P.62. 29 Seel St, L1. Metro: Liverpool Central. http://residenthotels.com. Set in a classic Ropewalks warehouse dating from the 1800s, *The Resident* has beautifully preserved the heritage aspects of the building in its reception areas. Sadly this doesn't extend to the rooms, which are more modern in design but very pleasant, with a stylish black-and-white colour scheme. There's no restaurant, but *Wreckfish Bistro* across the road does great breakfasts. **££**

Georgian Quarter

AACHEN HOTEL MAP P.72. 89–91 Mount Pleasant, L3. Bus: Rodney St. 0151 709 3477. Housed in a lovely Grade II-listed Georgian terrace, the German provenance of this three-star's name is something of a mystery but what's not in doubt is that this is a solid city-centre option at a good price. Rooms are rather old fashioned, with their floral bedspreads and wallpaper, but are homely enough and comfortable. They're made even better value by the inclusion of an all-you-can-eat breakfast, drawn from a wide menu of cooked and Continental options. **££**

BLACKBURNE ARMS MAP P.72. 24 Catharine St, L1. Bus: Falkner St. http://theblackburneliverpool.com. Offering the chance to stay above a traditional Liverpool pub, the *Blackburne Arms* has plain but pleasant guestrooms, with avocado walls, off-white tiled bathrooms, and tiny wall-mounted TVs. The food downstairs is consistently excellent, from the hearty full English breakfasts to the classic Sunday roasts. Prices can double or triple at weekends. **££**

ELYSIUM MAP P.72. 5 Rodney St, L3. Bus: Rodney St. http://elysiumliverpool.co.uk. In a graceful Georgian Quarter townhouse dating back to 1780, the Elysium offers comfortable serviced apartments which combine a generally modern decor – modish grey walls, wooden floors, bright, nature-themed wall art – with period features like original wooden beams. Apartments sleep six to ten and feature large lounge and dining areas, kitchens, and stylish en-suite bathrooms. **£££**

GEORGIAN TOWN HOUSE HOTEL MAP P.72. 60 Upper Parliament St, L8. Bus: South Hunter St. http://georgiantownhousehotel.co.uk. The name says it all, really: this is indeed a hotel in a Georgian town house, perfectly placed for exploring the Anglican Cathedral just across the road. The building is beautiful and the interiors have been upheld in a traditional style, with some lovely ornate mirrors and beautifully carved dark wood furniture. The only downside is that the shape of the house means the rooms vary a lot in size, so it's worth asking to see a couple. **££–£££**

HOPE STREET HOTEL MAP P.72. 40 Hope St, L1. Bus: Sugnall St. www.hopestreethotel.co.uk. One of Liverpool's finest boutique hotels, this modern property is at odds with its Georgian surroundings but does not feel incongruous. The facade is an angular collision of glass and wood, while the spacious rooms and suites are all pine furniture, light wood floors and exposed red brick walls. There's top notch British food on offer at the London Carriage Works downstairs (see page 78), while a sleek new spa should be open by the time you read this. **££–£££**

INTERNATIONAL INN MAP P.72. 4 South Hunter St, L1. Bus: South Hunter St. http://internationalinn.co.uk. Promising good value in what is generally an expensive part of town, *International Inn* is popular with backpackers and budget travellers. Small but comfortable four- to ten-bed dorms are available, while the self-described 'Cocoon Hotel' rooms offer more privacy and comfort. The TV and games lounge, complete with pool table, make this a good place to meet fellow travellers. **£**

Sefton Park & Lark Lane

GROVE SUITES MAP P.84. 7 Croxteth Grove, L8. Bus: Grove Park. 0151 264 9189, http://grovesuites.co.uk. For a cheaper option than many of the hotels near Sefton Park, this is a decent budget option and the sister property of *The Mountford* (see below). Rooms are simple but comfortable, with light wood floors, rugs and pine furniture, and tiled bathrooms. There's no restaurant here, but breakfast is available at *The Mountford* and the superb cafés and restaurants of Lark Lane (see page 92) are within walking distance. **£**

HALLMARK SEFTON PARK MAP P.84. 3 Aigburth Drive, L17. Bus: Aigburth Drive. 0330 028 3416, http://hallmarkhotels. co.uk. Housed in a grand old mansion on the edge of Sefton Park, the *Hallmark* was once the home of a wealthy cotton merchant. Today its 41 guestrooms nod to the building's heritage in their traditional design, with regal colour schemes of wine red and gold, but mod cons like wi-fi and TV. The *Hallmark Grill* serves superb afternoon teas and a classic British bistro menu, featuring curry, rump steak and lasagne. **£**

THE MOUNTFORD MAP P.84. 52 Croxteth Rd, L17. Bus: Ullet Rd. 0151 291 0509, http://themountfordhotel.co.uk. In a handsome redbrick building on the northern edge of Sefton Park, *The Mountford* has a traditional feel both outside and in. Hallways have black and white tiled floors and are lit by chandeliers, while in the lounge areas retro armchairs sit on Persian rugs. Guestrooms have a similarly classic design, with carved wooden beds, tasteful striped wallpaper, and spacious tiled bathrooms. Decent buffet breakfasts are available. **£**

SEFTON PARK HOTEL MAP P.84. 37 Aigburth Drive, L17. Bus: Mossley Hill Drive. 0151 727 7380, http://seftonparkhotel.co.uk. Just over the road from the southern tip of Sefton Park, some of the rooms at this traditional, well-run hotel overlook the park's picturesque boating lake. The rooms are not the biggest, but they're very comfortable, with pine furniture, TVs and pleasant en suites, while *O'Connor's Bar and Grill* is a lively Irish restaurant serving classic pub grub. **£££**

SEFTON VILLA MAP P.84. 14 Sefton Drive, L8. Bus: Ullet Rd. 0151 281 3687, http://seftonvilla.co.uk. In a big Victorian house still occupied by the owners and their family, this lovely B&B offers just one great-value guestroom, decked out in exquisite traditional style with a carved wooden bed, chandelier, and antique rugs and wall hangings. The en suite bathroom has a similarly old-school aesthetic, but despite the retro look, you'll find modern amenities like digital TV and wi-fi. Continental breakfasts are served overlooking the garden. **£**

SQUARE TREE HOUSE MAP P.84. Devonshire Rd, L8. Bus: Belvedere Rd. http://eleganthouseliverpool.com. Proudly claiming the title of Liverpool's smallest boutique hotel, *Square Tree House* is indeed small, with just five rooms in a converted townhouse near Princes Park. Each one is different, but all have a simple, tasteful design, with shuttered wooden wardrobes, antique rugs, and bathrooms decked in teal wood. Breakfasts are superb, with locally baked pastries, fresh fruit platters and salmon gravlax among the options. **££**

Further afield

BAYTREES 4 Queens Rd, PR9. Bus: Walton St. www.baytreeshotel.co.uk. It doesn't look like much, with its grey pebbledash exterior a picture of British suburban blandness, but this hotel's ordinary homeliness is its charm. In the comfortable reception room, with sofas clustered around a TV, you could be in a friend's living room, while the guestrooms are traditional but clean and very comfortable. **££**

THE BOLD 583 Lord St, PR9. Bus: Union St. http://boldhotel.com. Welcomed in by a striking carved wooden horse which rears above the entranceway, *The Bold* was extensively refurbished in 2020, and its 23 guestrooms are luxurious and stylish, with plush furnishings and a sleek grey and silver colour palette. Downstairs, there's a superb carvery and bar, with a breakfast buffet and the house speciality: a roast dinner wrapped in a Yorkshire pudding. **££–£££**

FORMBY HALL GOLF RESORT & SPA Southport Old Rd, L37. Metro: Freshfield. http://formbyhallgolfresort.co.uk. Set on 200 acres of green lawns, trees and lakes, this hotel is a relaxing spot, with modern, neutrally decorated rooms with large en-suites and golf course views; some ground-floor rooms have French doors which open onto the grounds. Golf is naturally high on the agenda here, with an 18- and nine-hole course, but if that's your idea of a good walk ruined, then there's also the pool, gym and supremely relaxing spa. **£££**

LEASOWE CASTLE Leasowe Rd, CH46. Metro: Wallasey Village. http://leasowecastle.com. If your idea of a dream British escape entails staying in a real-life country castle, look no further than this beautiful 1593 structure on the Wirral, which has at various times been a royal home, wartime prison, and now lovely hotel. You have a choice of the standard rooms, decked out in bright colours with modern furniture, or retro-style rooms with beautiful four-poster beds, deep wine-red carpets and vintage furnishings. **££**

LORD STREET HOTEL 178 Lord St, PR9. Bus: Union St. http://lordstreethotel. com. The luxurious Lord Street has just 17 guestrooms, each one different but all sharing a silvery colour scheme, with plush furnishings and Art Deco-style light fittings. The theme is continued elsewhere in the hotel, in the stylish lobby and the sleek champagne bar, which serves sparkling wines from across the world as well as a creative range of cocktails. Breakfast, lunch and dinner are on offer at *The Bold Hotel* across the road. **£££**

PHOENIX HOTEL 46 & 48 Foley Street, L4. Bus: Smith St. http://throstlesnesthotel. co.uk. In a historic red-brick Victorian building, the handsome Phoenix is well placed if you're visiting Liverpool or Everton's football grounds, being a few minutes' walk from each. The bedrooms are spacious and comfortable and have a classic yet modern look; some have Jacuzzi tubs. Classic full English breakfasts are on offer in the morning. **££**

THE VINCENT 98 Lord St, PR8. Metro: Southport. http://thevincenthotel.com. Sitting pretty on Lord Street, Southport's very own slice of Paris, *The Vincent* is an exercise in good taste from its Art Deco entrance sign up. Bedrooms have monochrome carpets, black marble surfaces and moody black-and-white photography adorning the walls, with spacious en-suite bathrooms with bathtubs and showers. The bar and restaurant follow a similar aesthetic, and serve exquisitely crafted cocktails and an eclectic food menu, from sirloin steak to sashimi platters. **£££**

ESSENTIALS

Liverpool Lime Street station

Arrival

By plane

Liverpool John Lennon Airport is 12km southeast of the city centre, near Speke Hall. The eleventh busiest airport in the UK in 2021, it serves as a hub for travel to the northwest, but is not as big or busy as Manchester Airport. International flights to Liverpool are mostly from within Europe, with the exception of Morocco – Ryanair (http://ryanair.com) flies here from Marrakesh, as well as from Madrid and Ibiza in Spain, Rome in Italy, and Warsaw in Poland. EasyJet (http://easyjet.com) fly between Liverpool and Amsterdam, Paris and Nice, among other destinations in France. The same airline connects Liverpool with several destinations in Turkey. From Spain, EasyJet also flies from Barcelona and Alicante to Liverpool. Wizz Air (http://wizzair. com) connects Liverpool with Gdansk in Poland and Budapest in Hungry. Other countries with airports that fly to Liverpool include Greece, Croatia, Hungary, Austria, Denmark, Sweden, Ireland, Malta and Portugal.

By train

The main train station serving Liverpool's city centre is Liverpool Lime Street, which sits in the historic St George's Quarter; opened in 1836, it is the oldest grand terminus mainline railway station in the world. Lime Street connects the city with Birmingham, Manchester, Leeds, Newcastle, London Euston, Chester and Blackpool North. Train companies running services into and out of the station include Mersey Rail (http://merseyrail.org), Northern (http://northernrailway.co.uk), and Transport for Wales (http://tfwrail.wales). A five-minute walk south of Lime Street, Liverpool Central connects Liverpool with other destinations in the north, including Southport, Kirby and Chester, via Merseyrail. Both of these train stations are in the heart of the city centre, and many hotels and attractions can be reached on foot; otherwise, both are also connected to the local Merseyrail train network, and to local bus routes.

By bus

Two major bus companies connect Liverpool to other cities in the United Kingdom: National Express (http://nationalexpress.com) and Megabus (http://uk.megabus.com). Destinations include London, Manchester, Birmingham, Cardiff, Glasgow, Leeds and Leicester. Long-distance buses arrive at the Liverpool ONE bus station, at Canning Place in the city centre.

By car

The main motorway connecting Liverpool with the rest of the country is the M62, which goes east to Manchester, Leeds and Hull. This in turn connects to the M1, which goes south past Sheffield, Nottingham, Northampton and Milton Keynes to London. Liverpool is connected by road to the Wirral Peninsula via the Kingsway and Queensway tunnels. To the north, the M6 runs towards Preston, Lancaster and Carlisle, becoming the A74(M) near the border with Scotland.

Getting around

Liverpool's city centre is compact, and most of it is navigable on foot. A guided walk is a great way to get a feel for the city while learning about its history; Liverpool Famous Walking Tours (www. liverpoolfamouswalkingtours.com) are a well-regarded operator.

For those with reduced mobility, however, or to travel further afield, there are numerous transport options available. Liverpool's traffic is relatively light compared to bigger cities like London and Manchester, and renting a car can be a good option. Sixt (http://sixt.co.uk), Europcar (http://europcar.co.uk) and Easirent (http://easirent.com) have outlets at Liverpool John Lennon Airport; Enterprise also have an office at 402 Queens Dock, Norfolk St in the city centre.

Taxis are plentiful in Liverpool. Black Hackney carriages can be flagged everywhere and are a comfortable but more expensive way to get around; alternatively, call a trusted local company like ComCab (http://comcab.co.uk). Uber (http://uber.com) is available across Liverpool and is invariably cheaper and quicker than using a traditional taxi service.

Liverpool and the surrounding area is connected by the Merseyrail train network (http://merseyrail.org), which runs on three lines (Northern, Wirral and City), partly underground, and connects 68 stations. Merseyrail is a convenient way of getting between Liverpool city centre and outlying places of interest, including Crosby, Southport and Port Sunlight. Route information and status updates can be found online and on the Merseyrail app, though standard tickets, rather frustratingly, can only be purchased at the station. If you'll be making several journeys in one day, it's worth buying a Day Saver, which can be purchased online. Family tickets include unlimited travel for one day, for one or two adults with children aged 5–15.

The most extensive local transport option is the Merseytravel bus network (http://merseytravel.gov.uk), which covers hundreds of bus stops across the city. The main city centre terminuses are Liverpool ONE and Queen Square. The one-day Solo Ticket allows for unlimited bus travel on the network.

Liverpool's relatively compact size makes cycling an appealing way of getting around. A cycling map showing routes and bicycle parking can be found at http://visitliverpool.com. The CityBike share scheme allows you to rent bicycles for £1 per hour, picking them up at one hub and dropping them off at another.

The most enjoyable way to travel between Liverpool and the Wirral Peninsula is on the iconic Mersey Ferry (http://merseyferries.co.uk), which operates both as a tourist attraction (see page 39) and a means of public transport. The commuter service only runs Mon–Fri 7.20–9.40am and 5–6.40pm between Pier Head in Liverpool and Seacombe on the Wirral.

Directory A-Z

Addresses

Addresses are written in the form "8 Dale St, L2", with L2 being the postcode area. House and building numbers in the UK tend to jump across the street, so one side will have numbers 1, 3, 5 etc while 2, 4, 6 etc will be found opposite them.

Children

Liverpool is very child-friendly, and children are welcome in nearly all restaurants and cafés, with many offering dedicated children's menus. The exception to Liverpool's child-friendly spaces are bars (and, obviously, nightclubs) which will generally insist on an over-18 only policy – the same is true of some pubs, although many pubs allow children who are accompanied by adults.

Cinema

Mainstream films are shown at chain cinemas and multiplexes across the city, while art house, indie and foreign-language films are also shown at cultural centres like FACT (see page 61). Film listings can be found online at http://odeon.co.uk. For a more deluxe film experience check out the Everyman Cinema at 35 Victoria St (http://everymancinema. com), where a historic building houses a bar, restaurant and plush auditorium where you can sit back on sofas to enjoy the film.

Crime and emergencies

Violent crime against tourists is extremely rare in the UK, but petty theft, mugging and pickpocketing are more common – you're unlikely to be affected, but it pays to be vigilant. The rules are the same as anywhere else: don't flash cash or expensive jewellery or gadgets, keep hold of your bags, and make sure you're aware of items in your pockets.

Discount passes

Most of Liverpool's museums are completely free, including some of the most famous like the Tate (see page 34) and the World Museum (see page 25). Most paid attractions offer discounted rates for children, students, and senior citizens, and further discounts can be had by buying the Liverpool Pass (buy online at https://liverpoolpass.co.uk/passes) which includes unlimited access to the British Music Experience, River Explorer Cruise, City Explorer Liverpool, Strawberry Field, The Liverpool FC Story Museum and the Beatles Story.

Electricity

Like the rest of the UK, Liverpool uses three-pin type G plugs, and the current is 230V AC. North American appliances will need a transformer and adaptor; those from Europe, South Africa, Australia and New Zealand only need an adaptor. Increasingly, modern hotels may have USB mains plug sockets, though you should not rely on this.

Embassies and consulates

Italy, 2nd Floor 14 Water St T James St, 0151 305 1060.
Spain, Gladstone House 2 Church Rd T Mossley Hill, 0151 734 6532.
Germany, 5th Floor Hanover House, Hanover St T Liverpool Central, 07757 372 641.
Netherlands, c/o Mersey Maritime Maritime Knowledge Hub, 3 Vanguard Way, Birkenhead, 0151 231 2957.

Health (doctor, dentist, emergencies, 24hr pharmacy)

Pharmacists (known as chemists in England) can advise you on minor conditions but can dispense only a limited range of drugs without a doctor's prescription. Most are open roughly 9am–7pm, though some are open later; the Tesco Extra at 215 Park Rd has a pharmacy open until 10.30pm. For generic pain relief, cold remedies and the like, the local supermarket is usually the cheapest option.

Internet

Most hotels and hostels in Liverpool have free wi-fi. In addition, many museums, public buildings, tourist offices and some train stations provide free wi-fi, as do numerous cafés, restaurants and bars. Increasingly less common are dedicated internet cafés, but some public libraries also offer free access. Many public wi-fi networks extend into public streets, such as the free wi-fi offered by Liverpool ONE.

LGBTQ travellers

England offers one of the most diverse and accessible LGBTQ scenes anywhere in Europe. Nearly every sizeable town has some kind of organized LGBTQ life, and Liverpool is no different. Listings, news and reviews can be found at *Gay Times* (http://gaytimes. co.uk) and Pink News (http://pinknews. co.uk). The website of the campaigning organization Stonewall (http:// stonewall.org.uk) is also useful, with directories of local groups and advice on reporting hate crimes, which, unfortunately, continue to be a concern. The age of consent is 16.

Left luggage

Liverpool Lime Street has Excess Baggage Co left luggage facilities opposite the ticket office (http://left-baggage.co.uk; 0151 909 3697). At 8 Gradwell Street in Ropewalks there is another left luggage facility, Store and Explore (0151 953 0003). Most hotels will also let you leave your bags behind reception, both before you check in and after you check out.

Lost property

To report lost or found property, contact Merseyside Police by calling 101 or at http://merseyside.police. uk. At Liverpool John Lennon Airport, lost property can be collected at the Information Desk (0871 521 8484, email: lostpropertylplairport@abm. com). Items lost on Liverpool's Mersey Rail train network are taken to the lost property office at James Street station (0151 955 2368, email: lostproperty@ merseyrail.org). Items lost at Lime Street station are held at the left luggage office; the lost property counter is open Mon–Thurs 7am–9pm, Fri–Sun until 11pm. For items left on trains, contact the relevant train company.

Money (including ATMs, banks, costs, credit cards, exchange)

England's currency is the pound sterling (£), divided into 100 pence (p). Coins come in denominations of 1p, 2p, 5p, 10p, 20p, 50p, £1 and £2. Bank of England notes are in denominations of £5, £10, £20 and £50. At the time of writing, £1 was worth US$1.22, €1.14, Can$1.66, Aus$1.82 and NZ$1.92. For current exchange rates, visit http:// xe.com.

The easiest way to get hold of cash is to use your debit card at an ATM; there's usually a daily withdrawal limit, which varies depending on the money issuer, but starts at around £250. You'll find ATMs everywhere in Liverpool, although they are fewer and

Price codes

Price codes for eating are based on a meal for one with a non-alcoholic drink:

£	£15 or below
££	£15–30
£££	£30–45
££££	£45 and above

Price codes for accommodation are based on a double room, including breakfast, unless otherwise stated:

£	£50 and below
££	£50–100
£££	£100–£200
££££	£200 and above

further between in suburban areas; look for banks and newsagents.

Credit cards are widely accepted in hotels, shops and restaurants – MasterCard and Visa are almost universal, charge cards like American Express and Diners Club less so.

Paying by plastic involves inserting your credit or debit card into a "chip-and-pin" terminal, beside the till in shops, or brought to your table in restaurants, and then keying in your PIN to authorize the transaction. Contactless payments, where you simply hold your credit or debit card on or near a card reader without having to key in a PIN, are prevalent for transactions for up to £30 at the time of writing. Note that the same overseas transaction fees will apply to contactless payments as to those made with a PIN. Contactless has increased the number of establishments that take card – even market stalls may do – though some smaller places, such as B&Bs and shops, may accept cash only, and occasionally smaller shops and pubs charge a minimum amount for card payments (£5 or £10 usually).

You can change currency or cheques at post offices and bureaux de change – the former charge no commission, while the latter tend to be open longer hours and are found in most city centres and at the airport and train stations.

Opening hours

Though traditional office hours are Monday to Saturday from around 9am to 5.30pm or 6pm, many businesses, shops and restaurants in Liverpool, as throughout England, will open and close at different times. The majority of shops are open daily, but some places – even the so-called "24hr supermarkets" – are closed or have restricted hours on Sunday. Banks are not open at the weekend. We have given full opening hours for everything we review – museums,

galleries and tourist attractions, cafés, restaurants, pubs and shops, noting where they're especially complex or prone to change and you should check before visiting. While many local shops and businesses close on public holidays, few tourist-related businesses observe them, particularly in summer. However, nearly all museums, galleries and other attractions are closed on Christmas Day and New Year's Day, with many also closed on Boxing Day (Dec 26). England's public holidays are usually referred to as bank holidays (though it's not just the banks who have a day off).

Phones

The prefix 07 is for mobile phones/cellphones. UK landlines are prefixed with an 'area code'; most of the numbers you'll see in this Guide begin with Liverpool's area code, 0151. However you'll also see 01704 for Southport, 01244 for Chester and 0161 for Manchester.

For directory enquiries, there are numerous companies offering the service, all with six-figure numbers beginning with 118, but charges are extortionate (with minimum charges of £5 plus and costs quickly escalating) and so best avoided. Numbers and addresses in the public domain can be found at http://192.com.

Most hotel rooms have telephones, but there is almost always an exorbitant surcharge for their use. Public payphones – telephone boxes – are still found, though with the ubiquity of mobile phones, they're seldom used.

To use your mobile/cellphone, check with your provider that international roaming is activated – and that your phone will work in the UK. Any EU-registered phones will be charged the same rates for calls, text messages and data as your home tariff. Calls using non-EU phones are still unregulated and can have prohibitively expensive roaming charges. If you're staying in England for any length of time, it's often easiest to buy a local SIM card in the UK.

Post offices

The British postal service, Royal Mail, is pretty efficient. First-class stamps to anywhere in the UK currently cost 95p and post should arrive the next day; if the item is anything approaching A4 size, it will be classed as a "Large Letter" and will cost £1.45p; if you want to guarantee next-day delivery, ask for Special Delivery (from £6.85). Second-class stamps cost 68p, taking up to three days; airmail to the rest of Europe and the world costs from £1.85 and should take three days within Europe and five days further afield. Stamps can be bought at post offices, but also from newsagents, many gift shops and supermarkets, although they usually only sell books of four or ten first-class UK stamps. To find out about your nearest post office, see http://postoffice.co.uk.

Smoking

Smoking is banned in all public buildings and offices, restaurants and pubs, and on all public transport. In addition, the vast majority of hotels and B&Bs no longer allow it. E-cigarettes are not allowed on public transport and are generally prohibited in museums and many other public buildings; for restaurants and bars it depends on the individual proprietor so if in doubt, ask.

Time

Greenwich Mean Time (GMT) – equivalent to Coordinated Universal Time (UTC) – is used from the end of October to the end of March; for the rest of the year Britain switches to British Summer Time (BST), one hour ahead of GMT.

Tipping

Although there are no fixed rules for tipping, a 10 to 15 percent tip is anticipated by restaurant waiters. Tipping taxi drivers ten percent or so is optional, but most people at the very least round the fare up to the nearest pound. Some restaurants levy a "discretionary" or "optional" service charge of 10 or 12.5 percent, which must be clearly stated on the menu and on the bill. However, you are not obliged to pay it, and certainly not if the food or service wasn't what you expected. It is not normal to leave tips if you order at the bar in pubs, though more likely if there's table service in bars, when some people choose to leave a few coins. You may well also see a tip jar on the bar at cafes and pubs, although there is never any pressure to contribute. The only other occasions when you'll be expected to tip are at the hairdressers, and in upmarket hotels where porters and bell boys expect and usually get a pound or two per bag or for calling a taxi.

Toilets

In the last twenty years, the number of public toilets in the United Kingdom has dropped by a third due to public spending cuts. However, at the same time there has been a rise in the number of high street cafes, which nearly all have toilets but only for the use of paying customers. The handy website The Great British Public Toilet Map (http://toiletmap.org.uk) is a useful website for helping people locate their nearest public toilet – aimed particularly at the young, elderly and those with medical conditions.

Tourist information

There are three main tourist information centres in Liverpool and the surrounding area. The first is within the Magical Beatles Museum at 23 Mathew Street (0151 233 6800, email: liverpoolvisitorcentre@liverpool.gov.uk; Mon–Sat 10am–4.30pm). The second is at Southport Library in the Atkinson building on Lord Street (0151 934 2118, email: Southport.Library@sefton.gov.uk; Mon–Sat 10am–5pm). There is another tourist information centre at Liverpool Central Library at 1840 William Brown St (0151 233 3069; Mon–Sat 10am–4.30pm). All are helpful and happy to provide information, recommendations and maps.

Travellers with disabilities

All new public buildings in the UK – including museums, galleries and cinemas – are obliged to provide **wheelchair access**; airports and (generally) train stations are accessible; many buses have easy-access boarding ramps; and dropped kerbs and signalled crossings are the rule in every city and town. According to disability resource Euan's Guide, Liverpool was one of the UK's most accessible cities for disabled travellers in 2018. The city has also done well to overcome the accessibility challenges posed by its Victorian architecture. Major museums, including the World Museum, Museum of Liverpool and Merseyside Maritime Museum, are accessible by wheelchair on every floor and feature hearing aid assistance. Liverpool and Everton football clubs both feature designated seats for visitors with impaired mobility. An increasing number of hotels are wheelchair-friendly. Discounts are available for disabled passengers on the UK's rail network, even if you do not hold a Disabled Persons Railcard; details can be found at www.disabledpersons-railcard.co.uk.

Useful resources for travellers with disabilities include Accessable (http://accessable.co.uk) and Euan's Guide (http://euansguide.com), both of which allow you to search for restaurants, hotels and attractions by destination.

Festivals and Events

New Year's Day Proms

January 1
Liverpool Philharmonic Hall sees in the New Year with a concert of classical favourites; expect British classics like Elgar's *Land of Hope and Glory* and *Nimrod*.

Chinese New Year

Late Jan/Early Feb
Processions, fireworks and festivities mark the Chinese New Year in Liverpool's Chinatown with a bang. The city's Chinatown is extremely well-established and authentic, and is the oldest in Europe. A Chinese market, selling food and gifts, pops up on George Street.

Liverpool Beer Festival

Feb 16–18, http://camra.org.uk
The city's biggest beer festival is held in the atmospheric surroundings of the Lutyens Crypt beneath the Metropolitan Cathedral, with hundreds of brews to sample.

St Patrick's Day

Mar 17
Liverpool's large Irish population – and virtually everyone else in the city – celebrates the much-loved Irish national holiday that is St Patrick's Day with a parade through the city centre, music and many, many pints of Guinness. A fun night out is virtually guaranteed.

Wirral Folk Festival

Mar 24–24, http://
wirralfolkonthecoast.com
The great and the good of the British
folk scene descend on the Wirral for
four days of music, food and camping.

Liverpool Comic Con

Apr 1–2, http://
comicconventionliverpool.co.uk
Fans of comics, cosplay, sci-fi and
everything pop culture descend on the
Exhibition Centre in King's Dock for
talks, stalls, photo ops and cast meets.

St George's Day

Apr 23
The day that commemorates England's
patron saint is celebrated – where
else – at Liverpool's St George's Hall.
The ornate St George stained-glass
window, usually off limits, is opened to
the public.

Liverpool Sound City

Apr 28–30, http://soundcity.uk.com
Leading music festival and conference
with gigs and workshops at venues
across the city centre.

River Festival

May 8–10, http://theriverfestival.co.uk
Liverpool's waterfront celebrates the
global gateway that is the Mersey with
art installations, music, dance, food
and wine – all completely free.

LightNight Liverpool

May 20, http://lightnightliverpool.
co.uk
A free one-night arts festival sees
the city's museums and galleries stay
open late for a special programme of
exhibitions.

Baltic Weekender

June 3, http://facebook.com/
balticweekender
Venues across the Baltic Triangle host
DJs, live musicians, and talks and
workshop sessions from those in the
creative and digital industries.

Liverpool International Music Festival

Mid-July, http://limfestival.com
Two days of music in Sefton Park, with
an eclectic line-up of pop, electronic,
funk and disco.

Heritage Open Days

2nd week Sept, http://
heritageopendays.org.uk
Annual opportunity to peek inside
more than 100 Merseyside buildings
that don't normally open their doors
to the public, from mosques to air raid
shelters.

Smithdown Festival

Oct 12–13
Historic Smithdown Road is taken
over by a free street party, with DJs,
live music, and pop-ups of some
of the city's favourite bars and
restaurants.

Halloween

Oct 31
Last day of the Celtic calendar and All
Hallows Eve: pumpkins, plus a lot of
ghoulish dressing-up, trick-or-treating
and parties, with many themed club
nights across Liverpool.

River of Light

Nov 1–9
Liverpool's waterfront blazes to life
with a nine-day riot of light, colour
and sound, with illuminated art
installations and fireworks.

Guy Fawkes Night/ Bonfire Night

Nov 5
Nationwide fireworks and bonfires
that draw the crowds. Guy Fawkes
commemorates the foiling of the
Gunpowder Plot in 1605 – atop every
bonfire is hoisted an effigy known as

the "guy" after Guy Fawkes, one of the conspirators.

Liverpool International Horse Show

Dec 30–Jan 2, http://liverpoolhorseshow.com
The M&S Bank Arena welcomes the planet's finest horses and riders for a four-day extravaganza of showjumping and stunt riding.

New Year's Eve

Dec 31
Big parties all over England; in Liverpool, there's outdoor parties at the *Kazimier Garden*, themed concerts at the Philharmonic Hall, and more.

Chronology

c. 70 Liverpool comes under the control of the Roman Empire, establishing their base at Deva Victrix, now known as Chester.

937 The Battle of Brunanburh may have been fought at Bromborough on the Wirral (the exact location is a matter of debate), considered the starting point of English nationalism.

1089 The Domesday book mentions the West Derby Hundred, a historic region which included the parish of Liverpool.

1190 Liverpool is known as 'Liuerpul', which means a muddy creek or pool.

c. late 900s The Irish document *Three Fragments* records a Norse settlement in the Wirral.

1207 King John declares the establishment of 'Livpul' and encourages people to move to the new borough, wanting to establish a port.

1229 A royal charter grants Liverpool merchants the right to form guilds.

c. 1235 Liverpool Castle is completed, built by the Earl of Derby.

c. late 1600s Liverpool begins to boom as a result of trade with new colonies in the Americas.

1644 Liverpool is besieged by Prince Rupert of the Rhine during the English Civil War. Parliamentarians take control of Liverpool and northern England.

1699 A ship, the *Liverpool Merchant*, departs for the West Indies carrying hundreds of slaves from Africa.

1715 The Thomas Steer's Dock is built, the world's first commercial wet dock.

1758AD The world's first subscription library is established, initially in private homes and then in the Lyceum.

1775–1783 Trade with the New World slows as a result of the American War of Independence.

1791 The world's first school for the blind is established in Liverpool.

1799 Liverpool's involvement in the slave trade reaches its peak, with 45,000 enslaved people trafficked through its docks.

1830 The Liverpool and Manchester Railway opens – the first intercity railway in the world.

1846 Construction finishes on the Royal Albert Dock, then the world's finest example of dock architecture and engineering.

1849 The first Liverpool Philharmonic Hall is built as a home for the Royal Liverpool Philharmonic Society.

1851 Liverpool's population reaches 300,000. Many of these are Irish immigrants fleeing from the Irish Potato Famine.

1854 The Neoclassical St George's Hall opens as a purpose-built events venue.

1870 Stanley Park is opened to the public; Sefton Park follows two years later.

1880 Liverpool is officially granted city status.

1881 The University of Liverpool is established, one of the country's original 'redbrick' universities, and the originator of that term.

1894 The Manchester Ship Canal is completed, allowing ships from the Irish Sea to travel from the Mersey Estuary direct to Manchester.

1911 The Liver Building opens – at the time, the tallest building in Europe.

1940–1942 The city undergoes heavy bombing during the Liverpool Blitz, becoming the most heavily bombed part of the country outside London.

1957 The Cavern Club opens on Mathew Street, originally as a jazz club – it would later go on to play a crucial role in the Merseybeat scene of the 1960's.

1961 The Beatles play their first gig at the Cavern Club on Mathew Street. They would go on to perform there nearly 300 times.

1967 Liverpool's strikingly modern Metropolitan Cathedral opens.

c. mid-1970s Liverpool's manufacturing industries decline, the docks close, and the city is plunged into a stark economic depression.

1978 Construction is completed on Liverpool's Anglican Cathedral, one of the biggest of its kind in the world.

c. mid-1980s Unemployment levels grow in Liverpool to some of the highest in the country.

1980 The world is shocked by the murder of John Lennon in New York City by a deranged fan, Mark David Chapman.

1989 96 people die during the Hillsborough stadium disaster during a match between Liverpool and Nottingham Forest.

c. mid-1990s Liverpool's economy begins to recover.

1999 Liverpool becomes the first British city outside London to be awarded Blue Plaques, designating buildings associated with significant historical figures and events.

2004 Liverpool's 'Maritime Mercantile City', centred around the waterfront, is awarded Unesco World Heritage Status.

2008 Liverpool is European Capital of Culture, kickstarting a new growth period in tourism and development.

2019 Liverpool Football Club lift the European Cup for a sixth time.

2020 The new Eureka! Mersey museum opens at Seacombe.

2022 The Shakespeare North Playhouse opens in Prescot.

2023 The city hosts the Eurovision.

SMALL PRINT

Publishing Information
Second edition 2023

Distribution
UK, Ireland and Europe
Apa Publications (UK) Ltd; sales@roughguides.com
United States and Canada
Ingram Publisher Services; ips@ingramcontent.com
Australia and New Zealand
Booktopia; retailer@booktopia.com.au
Worldwide
Apa Publications (UK) Ltd; sales@roughguides.com
Special Sales, Content Licensing and CoPublishing
Rough Guides can be purchased in bulk quantities at discounted prices. We can create special editions, personalised jackets and corporate imprints tailored to your needs. sales@roughguides.com.
roughguides.com

Printed in Czech Republic

This book was produced using **Typefi** automated publishing software.

Rough Guide Credits
Editor: Kate Drynan
Cartography: Katie Bennett
Picture editor: Tom Smyth
Layout: Pradeep Thapliyal
Original design: Richard Czapnik
Head of DTP and Pre-Press: Rebeka Davies
Head of Publishing: Sarah Clark

Acknowledgements
Big thanks go to everyone I met in Liverpool whose help and hospitality made researching this book so enjoyable. In particular, I'd like to thank Sophie Shields, Lucy Noone Blake, Joe Keggin and Lucy Nixon, Marcos Magalhaes, Charlotte Winby, Christine Whittle, Dominic Beaumont at Tate Liverpool, Laura Garner, and my editors Sarah Clark and Kate Drynan at Rough Guides.

Author biography

Daniel Stables is a travel writer and journalist based in Manchester. He writes about Asia, Europe, the Americas and the Middle East, and has worked on over a dozen Rough Guides titles and for various websites and magazines. His work can be found at his website, http://danielstables.co.uk, on Twitter @DanStables, and on Instagram @danstabs.

Help us update

We've gone to a lot of effort to ensure that this edition of the **Pocket Rough Guide Liverpool** is accurate and up-to-date. However, things change – places get "discovered", opening hours are notoriously fickle, restaurants and rooms raise prices or lower standards. If you feel we've got it wrong or left something out, we'd like to know, and if you can remember the address, the price, the hours, the phone number, so much the better.

Please send your comments with the subject line "**Pocket Rough Guide Liverpool Update**" to mail@uk.roughguides.com. We'll credit all contributions and send a copy of the next edition (or any other Rough Guide if you prefer) for the very best emails.

Photo Credits

(Key: T-top; C-centre; B-bottom; L-left; R-right)

Alamy 103

Getty Images 12T, 16B, 51, 54, 96

Hilton 112/113

iStock 2BL, 4, 11T, 17B, 19B, 20B, 28, 60, 71, 83, 88, 100, 102

Leonardo 56

Mark McNulty 26

Marketing Liverpool 12B, 13, 14B, 16T, 21B, 23, 25, 35, 47, 57, 67, 69, 77, 78, 81, 94, 120/121

Shutterstock 1, 2TL, 2MC, 2BC, 5, 6, 10, 11B, 13, 14T, 15B, 15T, 17T, 18T, 18C, 18B, 19T, 19C, 20T, 20C, 21T, 21C, 29, 31, 32, 38, 39, 40, 41, 42, 45, 48, 49, 53, 58, 59, 63, 65, 74, 75, 76, 80, 82, 87T, 87B, 89, 90, 92, 97, 98, 99, 101, 104, 107, 108, 109, 110

ReptOn1x at Wikimedia Commons 93

Index